Your Horoscope 2023

....

Aries

21 March – 20 April

igloobooks

igloobooks

Published in 2022
First published in the UK by Igloo Books Ltd
An imprint of Igloo Books Ltd
Cottage Farm, NN6 0BJ, UK
Owned by Bonnier Books
Sveavägen 56, Stockholm, Sweden
www.igloobooks.com

0722 001
2 4 6 8 10 9 7 5 3 1
ISBN 978-1-80108-398-0

Written by Sally Kirkman
Additional content by Belinda Campbell and Denise Evans

Designed by Richard Sykes
Edited by Katie Taylor

Printed and manufactured in China

CONTENTS

· · · · · · · · · · · · · · · ·

INTRODUCTION
·················

This 15-month guide has been designed and written to give a concise and accessible insight into both the nature of your star sign and the year ahead. Divided into two main sections, the first section of this guide will give you an overview of your character in order to help you understand how you think, perceive the world and interact with others, and – perhaps just as importantly – why. You'll soon see that your zodiac sign is not just affected by a few stars in the sky, but by planets, elements and a whole host of other factors, too.

The second section of this guide is made up of daily forecasts. Use these to increase your awareness of what might appear on your horizon so that you're better equipped to deal with the days ahead. While this should never be used to dictate your life, it can be useful to see how your energies might be affected or influenced, which, in turn, can help you prepare for what life might throw your way.

By the end of these 15 months, these two sections should have given you a deeper understanding and awareness of yourself and, in turn, the world around you. There are never any definite certainties, but with an open mind you will find guidance for what might be, and learn to take more control of your own destiny.

THE CHARACTER OF THE RAM

First in the zodiac year, first to get up in the morning, first to lend a helping hand and probably first on school sports days; Arians are a bundle of magnetic energy and quick-fire ideas. They tend to be the charismatic leaders of their pack, even if they don't volunteer themselves for the job. Whatever adventure Arians choose to chase after, there will always be a queue of admiring followers turning to these lively trendsetters for inspiration. Arians are aspirational and unparalleled in their zest for life, creative ideas and ability to get what they want.

Born in spring at the start of the equinox, the life and energy of Arians is palpable. It germinates in their abundance of ideas, flowers in their extrovert behaviour and bursts into life through their sometimes-impulsive actions. For Arians, the beginning of any venture is where their excitement lives and, sadly, often also dies. Whilst Arians thrive on beginning projects, whether it's starting up a business or learning a new craft, they don't always have the patience to see it through, leaving a path of half-painted canvases, unfinished novels and dust-gathering roller skates in their wake. It's not that Arians are ones to give up as such, far from it, but their childlike energy and impulsiveness can often become an impatient restlessness if a certain endeavour isn't going their way as quickly as they'd like it to. When one has as many fantastic ideas as Arians do, it's easy to understand why they may choose to ditch one enterprise to pursue another newer and 'greener' one. Although this quick-burning fire of interest can be problematic in love for Arians, resulting in short-lived lusts, their dependability is generally what they are better known for. When a problem occurs and someone suggests 'I know a person who can help with that', that person is likely to be an Arian.

THE RAM

Despite being born in springtime, there's not too much that's lamb-like about Arians! The Ram is known for being headstrong, and uses its impressive horns to settle arguments until it finally wins. Arians do not like losing an argument and so rarely stop until they eventually win. It all comes back to being first because, as Arians would argue, what other outcome is there? This fighting quality has its pros and cons. Professionally, especially with those who are self-employed, the competitive, cardinal nature of Arians can be a vital characteristic for coming out on top. It's important for Arians to be aware of their combative nature in their personal relationships, too. It's vital that they learn to identify when a win for someone else is equally a win for them. This will help to keep their relationships happy and long-standing. The Ram is wild, ruling and sometimes angry, and it's these shared qualities that can make Arians so alluring to others, and viewed as a challenge or a chore to keep up with.

MARS

It's probably no surprise that the fiery red planet of
Mars rules Aries. Named after the Roman god of war, Mars,
like the Aries sign, is often associated with passion and rage.
However, Arians, like war, can demonstrate strategy and
discipline just as much as they cause destruction and chaos.
Whilst Aries and Mars are closely linked to being red-hot and
ready to win a fight, there is more to both these parties than a
steamy appearance. Once past the attractive, bold-red of Mars,
it's key to note its comparatively small size in the solar system
and its proximity to Earth. These attributes make Mars known
as an inner or 'personal' planet. Similarly, whilst there may be
a lot to see on the surface of the charismatic, sociable side of
Arians, one might be mistaken for thinking that's all there is.
Despite being primarily extroverted, Arians tend to internalise
their deepest thoughts and feelings. They like to keep their
private lives just that, private. The apparent closeness but
inner mysteries of this planet and sign may be one of the
reasons why humankind is so captivated with the red planet
and Aries.

ELEMENTS, MODES
AND POLARITIES

Each sign is made up of a unique combination of three
defining groups: elements, modes and polarities. Each of these
defining parts can manifest themselves in good and bad ways
and none should be seen as a positive or a negative – including
the polarities! Just like a jigsaw puzzle, piecing these groups
together can help illuminate why each sign has certain
characteristics and help us find a balance.

ELEMENTS

Fire: Dynamic and adventurous, signs with fire in them can be extroverted. Others are naturally drawn to them because of the positive light they give off, as well as their high levels of energy and confidence.

Earth: Signs with the earth element are steady and driven with their ambitions. They make for a solid friend, parent or partner due to their grounded influence and nurturing nature.

Air: The invisible element that influences each of the other elements significantly, Air signs will provide much-needed perspective to others with their fair thinking, verbal skills and key ideas.

Water: Warm in the shallows and sometimes freezing as ice, this mysterious element is essential to the growth of everything around it, through its emotional depth and empathy.

MODES

Cardinal: Pioneers of the calendar, cardinal signs jump-start each season and are the energetic go-getters.

Fixed: Marking the middle of the calendar, fixed signs firmly denote and value steadiness and reliability.

Mutable: As the seasons end, the mutable signs adapt and give themselves over gladly to the promise of change.

POLARITIES

Positive: Typically extroverted, positive signs take physical action and embrace outside stimulus in their life.

Negative: Usually introverted, negative signs value emotional development and experiencing life from the inside out.

ARIES IN BRIEF

The table below shows the key attributes of Arians.
Use it for quick reference and to understand more about this fascinating sign.

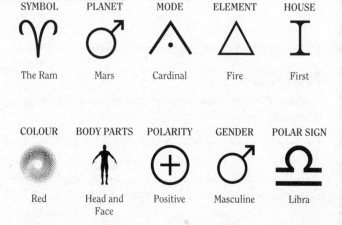

SYMBOL	RULING PLANET	MODE	ELEMENT	HOUSE
The Ram	Mars	Cardinal	Fire	First

COLOUR	BODY PARTS	POLARITY	GENDER	POLAR SIGN
Red	Head and Face	Positive	Masculine	Libra

ROMANTIC RELATIONSHIPS
. . . .

Warm, devouring, dangerous and exciting, the Aries element of fire perfectly enlightens a potential spouse as to what the fast-burning love of an Arian can feel like. To some, the attraction of Arians is obvious, which is why there will often be a queue lining up. For others, the liveliness and spontaneity of Arians can be too hot to handle. The difficulty with finding someone that thinks the Arian free spirit is inspiring rather than tiring is perhaps why they are not best known for having long-term relationships. Arians can find the start of romantic relationships exciting but short-lived if they find themselves unmatched in passion and energy.

For a long-term relationship to work, Arians must continue to feel free – free to follow their ambitions, to act on their spontaneity and to roam where their hearts desire. A partner for an Arian is someone who will acknowledge the need for adventure, as well as the Arian desire for independence. It's essential for an Arian's partner to have separate interests, not only to keep the Arian satisfied but also to not lose themselves. Arians are cardinal, which means they initiate the zodiac calendar and commonly initiate their romantic relationships. When Arians hold a flame for someone, they do not make a secret of it and are quick to act.

Not everyone has the same energy and vigour as Arians; in fact, some pride themselves on being the best. So how can they find an equal? Is an Arian only suited to another Arian? Although some feel that fire can only be fought with fire, this obvious solution may not be the best partnership of elements.

Regardless of signs, what Arians appreciate in a partner is someone who challenges them, shows a desire to share in their passions and, most importantly, brings humour into their lives.

ARIES: COMPATIBILITY 3/5

When a fire sign meets fire, there is sure to be lots of heat between the two. Whilst this could make for an exciting start, which both partners are sure to relish, it may be that they burn too brightly together and end up scalding each other. Both masculine and fire signs, these two are likely to share characteristics like leadership and ambition and will encourage one another to achieve their full potentials. Whilst passions and interests are likely to be shared, two Rams could end up butting heads too frequently to form a harmonious romance.

TAURUS: COMPATIBILITY 3/5

The Bull and the Ram may look like two headstrong individuals doomed to clash, but they actually have the potential for a sensual relationship. Whilst their passions for each other are intense, this couple will need to keep a reign on their potential stubbornness and desire to win in order to form a lasting relationship outside of the sheets. The Taurean can be guilty of possessiveness, which the free-spirited Arian may struggle with. However, with a joint love of nature and being outdoors, this duo could find their paradise together.

GEMINI: COMPATIBILITY 4/5

Though very different in their approaches to relationships, these two positive signs can bring out the very best in one another. Communication is key for any relationship and the Geminian's talkative nature can help the Arian vocalise their dreams and ideas. These two can form an intellectual bond that lays a strong foundation for their love. The Twins and Ram are both guilty of starting projects and not finishing them, which can extend to their relationship with each other, but their similarities and positive natures are likely to still see them part as friends if the romance extinguishes.

CANCER: COMPATIBILITY 1/5

This pair shares opposite characteristics that don't always attract, sadly. A homely creature, the Cancerian may find the Arian's adventurous roaming too uncomfortable and unsettling. Conversely, the Arian will not thrive in this relationship if constricted or held back in any way by the Cancerian. However, these water and fire signs are true opposites, and therefore can stand to learn a great deal from one another. In particular, the Cancerian can teach the Arian to be more considered before acting, whilst the Arian can teach the Cancerian to be less worrisome.

LEO: COMPATIBILITY 2/5

Arians are used to being first, but they'll have to learn to share the spotlight and decision-making if they fall for this leader of the jungle. These two signs should clearly recognise their similarities, and therefore know just how to advise and support one another in reaching their goals. With the Leonian led by the heart and the Arian by the head, arguments can be a roaring battlefield when these two don't see eye to eye. Ego and pride will need to be kept in check on both sides if this relationship is to go the distance.

VIRGO: COMPATIBILITY 4/5

There's not a lot that's similar about how an Arian and Virgoan think and approach their daily decisions. The Arian rushes in excitedly to almost everything, whereas the Virgoan needs to exhaust all the facts and options first. The Arian can teach the Virgoan the benefits of not getting too bogged down with decisions, and the Virgoan can teach the Arian the equal importance of noticing the smaller details in life. When these two team up, they will understand that they are very, very different, and will likely admire those differences in one another.

LIBRA: COMPATIBILITY 5/5

A polarity is complementary for any star-sign pairing. For an Arian, a Libran is the yin to their yang, the Sun to their Moon, the wind to their fire. Libra is an air sign, and can make the Arian's flames burn that much brighter. The Libran is best known for bringing harmony and balance into the world, and can make an ideal partner for the often-combative Arian. In this partnership of opposites, each can learn from the other in areas that they are lacking, with the Libran encouraging the Arian to communicate, and the Arian inspiring the Libran into action.

SCORPIO: COMPATIBILITY 2/5

If it's passion that an Arian desires in a relationship, Scorpio could be the perfect sign for romance. However, this match might be too combative for long-term happiness. Both ruled by the planet Mars, these two may come into this relationship armed and ready to fight. Scorpio's tendency to desire control of a situation could be a source of many explosive fights. If this fire and water sign can work out a balance of control and ease Scorpio's insecurities that, left unchecked, risk developing into jealousy, then they could have a steamy relationship rather than being left hot and bothered.

SAGITTARIUS: COMPATIBILITY 5/5

It will be a sure sign of Cupid's work if an Arian gets struck by one of the Sagittarian archer's arrows. This couple's compatibility is high due to their matching positivity and lively personalities. The Arian may have finally found their true match in the risk-taking Sagittarian. With a shared love of travel, there's unlikely to be any Arian adventure that the Sagittarian would pass up on. These two are go-getters and, if they can find shared interests, are an ideal match of two pioneering signs running off into the sunset together.

CAPRICORN: COMPATIBILITY 3/5

A Capricornian is not an obvious lover for an ambitious Arian, but shouldn't necessarily be ruled out entirely as a potential partner. The Capricornian usually takes much longer to size up a partner than the quick-working Arian, so patience will need to be exerted if this challenging relationship is to work. Like with any partnership in life, their differences can become their strengths. They should, however, be mindful of not wanting to change one another. Instead, the Capricornian and Arian should strive to make the other a better, more well-rounded person.

AQUARIUS: COMPATIBILITY 3/5

Two signs known for their admirable quality of being a good friend to all, an Arian and Aquarian should have a good solid foundation of friendship to base their romantic relationship on. This coupling of air and fire will always make for a fuelled relationship. Independence is key for keeping the Aquarian lover happy, so the Arian should be careful with trying to control the relationship or forcing the Aquarian to commit too soon. Whilst these two signs have many things in common, it will be discovering each other's differences that will be essential in keeping both partners interested in this relationship.

PISCES: COMPATIBILITY 2/5

A dreamy Piscean and action-lead Arian can learn a lot from one another, if they can find the impetus to do so. The Piscean often fears delving into the deep end of desires, generally choosing to back other's dreams over their own. The Arian will want to help the Piscean reach their full potential, but may unintentionally upset their extremely sensitive lover. However, the Piscean can use the same emotional side to offer much-needed support to the Arian, who often forgets to pause for thought. Together, they could form a considered connection, deeper than most.

FAMILY AND FRIENDS

Born in the first house of the zodiac calendar, symbolising the self and personality, Arians are known for their individuality. So where does that leave their family and friends? Arians love to offer both practical and physical support; putting up a shelf, booking a house viewing, mowing the lawn, getting people out of bed for marathon training (that they may or may not have signed everyone up for!). Arians are first to help others, and can be extremely encouraging and invested in seeing those closest to them realise goals. Family and friends will appreciate having Arians in their lives and acknowledge the positive influence they bring.

As siblings, Arians can be aspirational figures that their brothers and sisters look up to. This idolisation can manifest itself in numerous ways, such as copying their hairstyles or borrowing their clothes. Just be sure to ask Arians first before taking their things to avoid sparking their temper. Should Arians wish to start their own family and have children of their own, their approach to parenting will be fun and energetic. Arians will have no problem running around after young children, keeping up with their endless energy and behaving like big kids themselves. The ever-changing demands of parenthood would likely suit Arians by keeping them challenged, whilst satisfying their childlike and curious nature.

Arians do well in polar relationships, where others supply traits in which they themselves are lacking. However, what might be most important for any successful bond with Arians is having common interests. Sport is likely to be an area where Arians have hobbies, and they will often meet friends this way. Whether it's joining a sports club or competing in events,

FAMILY AND FRIENDS

. . . .

Arians' love for physical hobbies will steer them towards finding people with similar interests.

Another key characteristic of Arians is their need for freedom. This craving for independence will mean that travel is usually prevalent, whether it is for work or pleasure. This love of travel can mean that Arians have a far-reaching global network of family and friends. If Arians find that their work takes them away, it's key to seek close friendships where both sides have a strong sense of independence and will not feel abandoned. Life-loving Sagittarians and individualist Aquarians can make the best family and friends for any fast-paced Arians.

Friends of Arians will know that they are always in, whatever the plan. Their enthusiasm is instant and uplifting. Arians aren't likely to decline offers of fun, which can prove troublesome when they later realise they have double-booked themselves – again. Beware of being bumped to the rejection list if an Arian finds a better offer elsewhere. It's nothing personal. Arians often cancel plans without thinking they may be upsetting friends and family by doing so.

MONEY AND CAREERS

· · · · · · · · · · · · · · · · · ·

Being a particular star sign will not dictate certain types of career, but it can help identify potential areas for thriving in. To succeed in the workplace, it is just as important to understand strengths and weaknesses to achieve career and financial goals.

Arians are driven more by goals than money, which for some individuals may be one and the same, but in most cases will overlap in some ways. When someone succeeds in their professional field, which Arians generally do, being a high earner usually comes with the territory. So even if money was not the end goal for Arians, it is usually a by-product of success and passion.

Arians are typically competitive and overflowing with energy, which, if channelled at an early age, can make sports an obvious career path. Some Arians prefer the competition and sociability of team sports, and may choose to follow in the footsteps of many famous Arian footballers. Other Arians prefer the constant competition of self-improvement and find running a more satisfactory sport – just like Olympic gold medallist, Mo Farah.

Arians are self-starters. This go-getter initiative may materialise itself as a crowdfunding project, a hobby that turns into a business idea, or a mini side project that turns into a profitable company. Whatever career ladder Arians climb, they will scale it quickly and always reach the top of their profession. That is, of course, as long as the job at hand is able to satisfy their ambition, and Arians can see that their frequent ideas are being listened to and acted upon.

A job in which Arians feel stagnant or stifled is not one they will stay in for any great length of time. Arians work best when they have freedom, be it creatively or by working flexible hours, and may struggle to satisfy this need for independence in more traditional workplaces. Self-employment options may be a better fit for this me-first sign, allowing them to be their own boss, dictate their own hours and free themselves from the nine to five.

In a modern world of online influencers, such as Arians Casey Neistat and Zoe Sugg, the sky's the limit for pioneering individuals who aren't afraid to go after what they want. This digital age is perhaps the most exciting era for Arians, as it has given them an outlet that lets them work nomadically from coffee shops or mountaintops.

If drawn to a more traditional workspace, the me-first attitude will need to be dialled down. Lessening the need to constantly win and learning to be able to compromise is essential learning for Arians if they are to thrive – which fundamentally is what they want! That being said, any team that contains one or more Arians is likely to come out on top. Arians are practical problem-solvers and are first to help colleagues find the best solutions. This makes them generally very popular and an asset to any company.

As with family, colleagues cannot be chosen. Therefore, it can be advantageous to use star signs to learn about their key characteristics and discover the best ways of working together. Geminians can make for a helpful colleague by encouraging Arians to see a project from an alternative viewpoint. Geminians are also champion communicators, and can connect to Arians on an intellectual level and help them verbalise their ideas. Arians share a desire of winning with their fire sign relation, Leo. However, just like close families, these two know how to fight better than anyone and can make for argumentative teammates. As with any successful relationship, Arians should try to exercise patience and take a leaf out of the Geminian book about how best to communicate with colleagues or customers in order to thrive in professional endeavours.

HEALTH AND WELLBEING

· · · · · · · · · · · · · · · · ·

Arians are known for being one of the strongest and healthiest signs in the zodiac calendar. All associations with this sign, lively fire plus combative Mars mixed with the headstrong Ram, can equate to the makings of an energetic individual. It's important that Arians find ways of positively expelling this natural energy and one of the ways this can be done effectively is through sports. Arians are unlikely to be satisfied simply by running out their energy on a treadmill in the gym, rather this sign is more likely to enjoy team sports such as football or basketball to complement their social and competitive nature. Other Arians that feel the ruling of Mars more keenly may find that martial arts are their passion, like fellow Arian Jackie Chan.

Represented by the zodiac symbol of the Ram, this headstrong animal perfectly symbolises the ferocity and wildness in which Arians charge after what they desire most. The Ram is known not only for its strength, but also for having unbelievable balance on dizzyingly high and rocky terrains. This may be why some Arians find that their sense of adventure leads them to try thrill-seeking sports that rely on strength and balance, such as rock climbing, mountain biking or even aerial acrobatics. Whether Arians focus their abundance of energy and aptitude for action into a particular sport, their love for adventure is likely to have them craving after some sort of lifestyle in the great outdoors, whether that's hiking or wild swimming.

Physical activity is well suited to Arians, not only for the obvious benefits of keeping their bodies physically healthy, but also for their mental wellbeing. This highly charged sign needs a positive outlet for releasing their excess energy.

If Arians feel a fight boiling up in them, they would do well to throw their trainers on, step out of their front door into some fresh air and just run it out. Chances are they'll feel much better for having expelled some of their energy, especially applying it to something constructive, as this is what this positive sign naturally craves.

It's key for Arians to stay active in an area that brings them joy so as to avoid frustration, but this sign should be wary of pushing themselves too much and too quickly, as they could end up injuring themselves in the process. Slowing down, weighing up risks and taking a moment to simply breathe can help Arians maintain a positive state of mind. They would do well to try incorporating more meditative hobbies into their active lifestyles. Yoga will help stretch out overworked muscles and mediation will help calm a warrior-like approach to life, and bring a much-needed breath of tranquillity. Arians are traditionally linked to the head, and may find that they suffer from headaches more acutely and frequently, or conversely not at all. Either way, if Arians can periodically pause and calm their active mind and body, they could find it brings a clearer focus that leads to long-term health and happiness.

Aries

....

DAILY FORECASTS
for 2022

OCTOBER

Saturday 1st
If you are able to be selfless and consider a partner's needs, you may have a relatively easy day. Play by the rules and refrain from insisting on your own way. This may niggle you as you feel you aren't acting from your truth, but will be remembered when it matters.

Sunday 2nd
Mercury turns direct now. You might have a moment of utmost clarity or bewilderment. How you respond will depend on how you have presented yourself during the retrograde. Work and relationships still present challenges and can make you moody and resentful. Lie low and do nothing if you can.

Monday 3rd
Today you get a glimpse of your direction in life. You could be assessing past skills and talents and wondering how you can use them again. It may be possible to demonstrate one of these this afternoon. You could solve a money problem or a DIY project at home.

Tuesday 4th
You may be finishing up or scrapping a task at work. It's possible that you had a change of heart about it and realised it's not worth all the effort. You may have also looked at it through fresh eyes and seen it in a new light. This doesn't bother you.

Wednesday 5th

Genius ideas and solutions may be coming at you thick
and fast now. These may come from useful sources you had
previously dismissed. Lessons from your elders or bosses can
be beneficial and spur you into action. New inspiration may
come, and you can start networking on this.

Thursday 6th

Let your busy mind rest for a day or two. Go within and find
your centre of calm. The energy suggests that you enjoy a
moment or two of stillness before you rush back into the
outside world. Your dreams may send you messages worth
listening to.

Friday 7th

This is a great day to detox and declutter both your body
and your workspace. You may sign a new contract or similar
agreement and will need time to scrutinise it. Fortunately,
you have the right frame of mind to examine all the details
and look for hidden loopholes.

Saturday 8th

Your energy may be very low today. Take this as a hint to relax
and unwind. Your inner compass is right there in front of you,
so check in and see if it still suits you. There may be a small
tweak or two needed. Follow your heart today and don't listen
to your inner critic.

Sunday 9th

A full moon in your sign throws the spotlight on you. It's possible that you are celebrating a gain in status or a shift in dynamics at work. Pluto turns direct too which can help with any changes, new beginnings and permanent endings in your career.

Monday 10th

You may be extra busy now and taking advantage of the good energy in your sign. Efficiency and urgency are your middle names. An important conversation may be needed to determine your new daily duties. This may also be a medical appointment in which you get answers about your health.

Tuesday 11th

Mercury enters your relationship zone today. If conversations have been strained recently you may notice that this changes now. This could be a time where clandestine meetings or chats are exciting and prolific. Remember to listen as well as talk if you are getting to know someone new.

Wednesday 12th

Your day may begin with an emotional tremor. Something is brewing under the surface and it could be exciting you. Just remember not to steam ahead at your usual pace with this as you could spoil it all for yourself. Boundaries are important now if you desire to connect mutually.

Thursday 13th

Today comes with a warning. If you must talk about yourself, do be careful that you don't overdo it. You may come across as egotistic. Use active listening to show you are interested instead of responding with a statement which brings the conversation back to you. You may need to filter what you say.

Friday 14th

Saturn has a lesson for you today. You must consider your personal boundaries and how you wish to be treated in relationships. This should be your marker when offering to be partnered. Treat others as you would like to be treated and all will be well.

Saturday 15th

Emotionally, you may begin the day ready to grab what you desire with both hands. You may fear losing something you have now come to value and rely on. Spending quality time with family or in a cosy, safe setting will reassure you that this item or person needs handling with care.

Sunday 16th

You may feel at odds with a partner today because your needs are geared more towards your family. If you can involve them or bring them into the family circle, this can be resolved. This evening, you could be involved in discussions regarding money and your values. Gather your dearest around you.

Monday 17th

Review where the line starts and ends before you feel too smothered and need your own space. Recognising this may help to avoid unnecessary tension. You may crave alone time by evening. Give yourself enough space to detach from the family without causing a scene. They will understand.

Tuesday 18th

A burst of energy propels you in the direction of your lover. You could be in the mood for play and creativity. However, be careful that you don't bounce around too much and breach each other's comfort zone. You risk getting a bigger bounce back, which you may not know how to handle.

Wednesday 19th

The energy between Venus and Mars suggests that you can achieve a compromise or balance in your love life. As always, you need to ensure that you aren't being over-enthusiastic about the wrong things. You may desire to break a few rules, but this won't be a good idea.

Thursday 20th

This is a great day for making loving connections the main theme. From a position which asks you to stand up and speak your truth, you may hold both masculine and feminine energy equally. Health and unconditional relationships will also be in focus.

Friday 21st

Look at what you value for yourself and what is important to you in a partnership. You may find that you can meet in the middle and merge these with nice benefits. Enhancing a relationship by sharing your personal truths can make solid foundations and deep roots. Listen with an open heart to what your partner says.

Saturday 22nd

It may feel as if your inner compass is far away today, but look again. It may be that it's adjusting to your new north. Having learned how to pause and listen, you may see a new level developing that could change your ways of relating to others forever.

Sunday 23rd

Venus is in the heart of the Sun in your relationship zone. Make the most of this beautiful energy and invite love, beauty and harmony into your life. Saturn turns direct now too, and this will make things a little easier if you have been paying attention to his lessons.

Monday 24th

Your head and heart are perfectly in sync today. What's more, this happens in your relationship zone. You could be walking your talk now and showing that you mean every word you say. Heartfelt commitments can be made under this influence. You have a better idea of where you end and another begins.

Tuesday 25th

A new moon and solar eclipse throw a wild card on the table. The next two weeks could be intense and life-changing. Romance may get seductive and sexy, so arrange a weeknight with your lover. Alternatively, spoil yourself with some self-care and pampering. An impulse purchase won't hurt.

Wednesday 26th

It's possible that you get a visit from the past today. You could be in for a big surprise, which may excite or unsettle you. Remember what Saturn taught you about personal boundaries. You should not feel obliged to engage in a social activity with them if you're not comfortable with that.

Thursday 27th

How might you follow your true north out into the wider world? This may be on your mind today as you're outgoing and need more adventure in your life. You might feel like you are at the start of a race in which you walk, not run.

Friday 28th

You may revert to old habits today and surprise yourself. This could be a childlike sense of unfairness and you may have a tantrum or sulk in a corner. Maybe you have been told that you can't go somewhere and feel grounded. Maybe you just need to do some introspection.

Saturday 29th

A frustrating need to get something off your chest may lower the mood of the day. Take a leap of faith and speak. It may be that the person you need to talk to has the same questions. Your conversations can only go deeper if you are willing to take the first step.

Sunday 30th

Mars, your ruling planet, turns retrograde today. Now, more than ever, it's important that you slow down. Trying to push against the flow won't bring any results. As an Aries, this will be irritating and make your restless. Find new avenues for letting off steam and excess energy.

Monday 31st

If you are feeling personally attacked or criticised in the workplace, look at what has triggered you. You may be able to identify your own weak points now. These are likely to be about how you're always two steps ahead of the game. Self-control is necessary to work as a team.

NOVEMBER

· · · · · · · · · · · · · · · · · · ·

Tuesday 1st

Don't give up today. Keep moving forward and making progress, even if it's not at the speed you would like. You may face challenges concerning your social or interest groups. Question whether these are still in alignment with your personal truth. This energy will soon pass over.

Wednesday 2nd

Allow yourself to have a slow day and let your dreams carry you. You may be thinking about past loves today and this could trigger old wounds which need healing or soothing. Communications may not be going well at the moment, so withdraw and have some quality time for yourself.

Thursday 3rd

Today may be quite emotional, but in a nice way. You may have opened up channels to allow a deeper love to develop with a partner. The next few weeks are great for investigating your own psyche and how that can combine with a partner. This could be quite a journey.

Friday 4th

You may see your inner compass today, but this comes with a price. You may remember that this isn't the right time to be acting on your dreams. Try to minimise your plans into bite-size pieces that can be changed without too much trouble. Big plans aren't going to work.

Saturday 5th

Someone from your past is likely to reappear today. This could stir up feelings you'd rather not deal with. Maybe you've suppressed emotions and they are now bubbling to the surface. If this is a person in your present, open a discussion and resolve it together.

Sunday 6th

You may feel stuck in the middle of conversations today. It might be that you're the go-between or mediator. This is good energy, but you could be responsible for making the decisions. There is another possibility that the past comes back to haunt you now. Tread carefully and be kind to yourself.

Monday 7th

Planting seeds for future use may be possible. Anything that is on hold at the moment can be stored away safely. You may experience jealousy or manipulation within your friendship groups, and this might also involve a partner. Remember to put strong boundaries in place.

Tuesday 8th

A full moon and lunar eclipse may close the window on the weirdness of the last two weeks. Today's energy is intense, but propels you forward and leaves past ghosts behind. Listen for subtle messages or whispers from your psyche. Don't act or say something you may regret. Be an observer.

Wednesday 9th

You may be tempted to say something unkind today. Your mouth could run away with you if you aren't careful. Tricky energy can cause a revolt and show you where there is something wrong in your finances, values and possessions. Play the detective and figure this out.

Thursday 10th

It's possible that you run into trouble today with an elder or authority figure in your social groups. You may need to withdraw and have alone time later. This might be needed for you to process your childlike reactions in an adult way and discover why you respond the way you do.

Friday 11th

Today can be very frustrating for you. There may be some pent-up anger and irritability you need to express. Don't do it via conversations as this may not go well. Hard exercise, meditation or something you enjoyed as a child might be the answer. Try making messy art.

Saturday 12th

You may have a need for comfort and security from your precious loved ones this weekend. Time spent at home with your family may give you the support you need. Mothers and maternal figures, home cooking and safety zones could be the keys. Make a blanket tent and eat ice cream.

Sunday 13th

Stay in your nest today and work from there. This may give you time to think about things in a different way. You may be persuaded by a female family member that your responses were perhaps out of order. This may humble you and help you learn and grow.

Monday 14th

Step tentatively back out into the world and you may see that nothing was personal. This may have been an effect of Mars retrograde and you must now go easy on yourself. Self-love and care are something you should adhere to when feeling stuck. By afternoon, you may be more positive.

Tuesday 15th

Change is in the air and it may be happening with a close relationship. Try looking for more love and resetting the harmony with someone before taking any new steps. You might feel anxious about this, but it will be beneficial for all involved. Remember to use restless energy positively.

Wednesday 16th

Emotions can run deep today, and you may feel like processing these alone. Your voice isn't being heard right now, take this as a cue to listen to the voice inside you. If you have the time and energy, you can go as deep as you're comfortable with.

Thursday 17th

Think about your mental health now. There may be something bothering you that is affecting you in more ways than you realise. Reach out and broaden your horizons. Planning a future vacation or course of study could be the right next steps for you. Let your imagination free and travel to new lands.

Friday 18th

Today can be difficult as again you're restricted from moving ahead with your true north. You may have to be satisfied with making all the necessary plans and research for when the time is right to implement them. Get radical and plant seed thoughts. Watch how they grow.

Saturday 19th

You may be tired of doing nothing, but there are things you can do to appease your sense of adventure. A partner may help to create a vision board for a future together. It may be fun and bonding to study together. Foreign languages, philosophies and cultures could be your thing.

Sunday 20th

Partner time can be satisfactory today as you may be able to meet in the middle and appreciate each other's limits more. A sense of responsibility towards your partner may be reflected back at you. This could be a turning point, which deepens and matures the way you relate.

Monday 21st

You may be working up to discovering something intense and heartwarming. The lack of action and speed could be deepening your roots and respect for a lot of things. Sweet-talking in the late hours can provide inspiration and excitement, which will be mutual.

Tuesday 22nd

As the Sun shifts signs, you may get the boost you need to put holiday plans in place. You might be thinking about putting down a shared deposit, so be careful that this is equal or you could become resentful. You may be reminded of being let down in the past.

Wednesday 23rd

It's possible that you're having second thoughts about something, but this is perfectly natural and is a way of getting you to slow down and check every detail before committing. Forget past experiences and look at this through new eyes. You're not the same person you were then.

Thursday 24th

This is a great day for making that commitment. A new moon in your travel zone occurs whilst Jupiter turns direct. Emotionally, you are completely in tune with this energy and double blessed by planetary energy. This is the green light you've been waiting for. Go ahead and plan exciting things.

Friday 25th

You may feel tired today and enjoy some quiet activity. An emotional overload may have caught you by surprise. Your adrenals may be getting the same fix you experience through your natural energy outbursts, but the unusual source, emotions, have confused them. Rest and congratulate yourself on using energy wisely.

Saturday 26th

Today, you may feel certain that your life is headed in the right direction. Feelings of contentment can make the day go without any bumps. Allow yourself to relax and lap up this good vibe. You may wish to make a note of it and recall it when you feel down.

Sunday 27th

You can make changes today that may elevate your status and bring you more luck. It could be that you've found an ingenious way to nurture roots that take a long time to grow. A change of heart or attitude may allow you to see things differently.

Monday 28th

It can be easier to move through your day if you ask for support from friendship and interest groups. You may be more outgoing and willing to accept what others have to offer you. It's possible that you're still pushing against the flow, but when you realise this you may back off.

Tuesday 29th

The planetary energy today can make you optimistic and upbeat. Wise words from elders in your groups are there to help you progress. Listen well and adapt what you hear for your own purposes. You may need to rest and withdraw this evening as mental activity may have drained you.

Wednesday 30th

Don't let poor coping mechanisms affect your good progress.
You may default into bad habits today and feel bad about it
afterwards. Don't beat yourself up; this may be a small blip
where you relapsed into an older version of you. This evening,
you may be back to normal.

DECEMBER

Thursday 1st
Keep a low profile. There might be a lot of triggers coming up from your unconscious, which can be unsettling. Your inability to make progress may be bothering you more than you admit. A battle between the sexes may stir up long-held grudges. Hold on to your personal truth.

Friday 2nd
Although your busy mind may have kept you awake, a desire to do what you can, however small, powers you through the day. You may be a little selfish now, but this is self-protect mode and is good for you. Taking on chores in bite-size chunks can make you feel productive.

Saturday 3rd
There is lovely planetary energy for you to do weekend chores and meet up with people. Reach out to people you need to catch up with. Your interest and social groups may have festive activities lined up should you wish to join in. Be as outgoing as you can.

Sunday 4th

Neptune turns direct today. This is great news as you may now find a secure place to cling when contemplating your true north. You may notice that unrealistic dreams and plans will fall away and reveal the ones you are most likely to succeed in. Check the seeds you've planted.

Monday 5th

Today may feel like another new start. You might have tackled some demons from your unconscious and sent them packing. A more optimistic outlook aligns you with a vision of your onward path. This could be more practical and steadfast. You may now curb some impulses.

Tuesday 6th

If you have made travel plans, double-check that they are still right for you. There could be some doubts now as you take a fresh look at the value they hold. Communications at work will become a hotline for the next few weeks, so ensure you're meeting all your deadlines.

Wednesday 7th

This is a rare day where you can simply do what you need to and have time for your own things. You may notice that nobody demands anything from you and that your attention is perfectly on task. This may seem mundane, but you will notice the benefits.

Thursday 8th

A full moon sits with your ruler, Mars, today. Communications are highlighted and you may have a revelation or two via messages and emails. You may feel the urge for action, so make time for exercise. This moon may show completion of study or tie up loose ends and agreements.

Friday 9th

Settle in for a cosy weekend of feeding your soul. Family members, especially mothers or maternal figures, can give you a sense of safety. Alternatively, you may now step up as the nurturer of your clan. Give your mind a rest and see to your emotional needs today.

Saturday 10th

Women may step up and get the recognition they deserve now. You could be the one to highlight this. Restless energy may make you argumentative, but only in a way that brings out the compassionate warrior in you. Stand up for the underdogs today and you could be a hero.

Sunday 11th

Something may have dissolved from your unconscious and you now see it in its true colours. You may breathe a sigh of relief as you see how this can help you move on. You may notice a permanent ending as you leave this behind you. It's okay to grieve this loss.

Monday 12th

Your creative expression is what fuels you today. You may have a lot to say for yourself. This could be a technique you use to sort out what is in your head. If it comes out into the open, it's no longer churning around in your mind. Observe how you feel.

Tuesday 13th

Try not to go too far if you are currently making noises in some places. Your friendship and interest groups may not appreciate it. It's possible that you come across as a troublemaker. Say your piece and then withdraw for others to have time to process your words.

Wednesday 14th

Before the festive season keeps you busy, take some time to check in with your health and body. Is there something more you could be doing for yourself? You may like to declutter your surroundings, your office or your schedule. A healthy body needs a healthy mind and space.

Thursday 15th

The planetary energy is very grounded and practical today. This could weigh heavy on you as it's not natural for an Aries. Accept this as a day to get chores done. Making sure all is up to date will give you free time to concentrate on your own wants and needs.

Friday 16th

You may need to continue with doing practical things today. As much as you'd like to be dreaming up your biggest vision now, the time isn't right. Partner time is highlighted for the weekend, so if chores are done, your time is free. Achieve a balance between work and play if you can.

Saturday 17th

Going back to basics in a relationship could seem daunting.
It may be that you have reached a level of understanding where
roles have become seemingly mundane. Keep your flame
alive by sharing duties and responsibilities. Just because a
honeymoon period may be over, it doesn't mean you will have
less fun.

Sunday 18th

You may be more concerned with group ventures than with
one-on-one relationships. This could cause a bit of tension
but will soon be smoothed over. Don't turn your back on
something or someone unless you know that you can't go any
further with them.

Monday 19th

It could be that you do an about-turn and wish to reconnect
with a loved one. This may be a lovely reunion, or a mature
realisation has been reached. Above all, you wish to restore
the harmony you once had as you find it reassuring and
supportive in love relationships.

Tuesday 20th

Jupiter bounces back into your sign today and will stay there
for almost a year. There's no use in moaning about the past
now. This could be another turning point for you and will keep
you buoyant and optimistic through all challenges. Get busy
adding to your dreams and visions now.

Wednesday 21st

The winter solstice occurs today. This is a time to reflect on the year gone by and give gratitude where it's due. You may wish to reach out to long-distance friends and let them know you value them. An invite to travel may come your way today.

Thursday 22nd

You may be feeling the slowing down of the season. It could be easier for you now that everyone else is winding down too. A last minute work issue may give you a chance to show that keen mind of yours. You may come up with an ingenious way of ending the year.

Friday 23rd

A new moon in your career zone allows you to set early goals and intentions for your work. You may be starting a new project which will take time and effort. Long term goals can be evaluated or set in motion now. Slow and steady progress will be required.

Saturday 24th

The excitement of the season is filling your heart and mind. You may have a deep desire to see that everyone is happy and informed. Taking a leadership role here can make you show off your very best side and keep you in line with your true path and purpose.

Sunday 25th

As long as everyone knows their roles and keeps to them, you can maintain discipline today. If you're entertaining, it could be you needing to stay controlled. Selflessness can be the theme of the day and will lift everyone's spirits. Enjoy this festive day wherever you are.

Monday 26th

Tensions may be rising today as you could be wishing to connect with people who are otherwise disposed. Perhaps you can check in with some online friends and groups. The holiday season may have lost its sparkle as you could be feeling too confined at home and need to break free.

Tuesday 27th

A time for solitude presents itself and you may accept it willingly. You may find a spiritual outlet supports your needs. Take this precious time to consider all that you have uprooted and dealt with this year. Congratulate yourself and look forward to watching all you've planted grow.

Wednesday 28th

This is a great day for dreaming. Your energy may be too low to do anything more. Concentrate on your true north and what you want from life next year. Your career, status, romance and quality of life are key themes you use today to align with your own values.

Thursday 29th

Mercury turns retrograde today in your career zone. If you have something new happening at work, try to buy yourself some time for three weeks. It may go against everything you have dreamed and learned if you rush into something in the new year. Be proud of any offer that comes along.

Friday 30th

It may be difficult to do your own thing today and this will irritate you. You may be dragged out to events which don't appeal. Keep a low profile if you must. Try not to exaggerate any bad mood as it could possibly turn into a hot-headed argument you could do without.

Saturday 31st

You could be missing out if you are sulking in your room. As the day progresses, you shed some heavy weight and come out to party. Spending time reflecting on the experiences of the last year will give you the space you need to look forward to the new year, and all its opportunities for growth.

Aries

. . . .

DAILY FORECASTS
for 2023

JANUARY

· Sunday 1st ·

Focus your attention on work and money as the new year begins. Find a role model in your life and their influence could help you make swift progress. It's time to ring the changes when it comes to earnings. Be independent and don't rely too heavily on your partner.

Monday 2nd

Even though it's a Bank Holiday, you're wise to line up some new intentions for your career or future path. Visualisation techniques could offer inspiration. It's a promising date to voice your intentions out loud. Offer a request up to the universe to manifest your dreams.

Tuesday 3rd

Love planet Venus enters your friendship zone today. This means that love and friendship are linked over the next few weeks. If there's someone you would like to reconnect with, today's stars are promising for reaching out to past connections, friends and colleagues.

Wednesday 4th

Luck could come your way through your friendships and group alliances, so ensure you have the right people on your side. If you're married or in a long-term relationship, aim to be best friends with the one you love. If you're single, ask a friend for an introduction to a potential match.

Thursday 5th

Think of this time of year as a gestation period when you're drawing up new ideas, having key conversations and thinking about what to do next. Trust your intuition with an important home or work decision. Take a different route in life and you could revolutionise your earning potential.

Friday 6th

Today's full moon lights up the foundations of your horoscope. You may be juggling home and work, family and career more than usual. If a new opportunity comes your way, take your time deciding whether it's right for you. The turning point comes close to January 18th.

Saturday 7th

You may want to nest this weekend or hang out with your family. Sometimes it's hard to step out of your comfort zone, even when you're being called to do so. Try not to be overly extreme and go too far in any one direction; instead, seek a harmonious work/life balance.

Sunday 8th

You may be ready to venture out today and have some fun. Be with the people in your life who lift your spirits and open your heart. If you've been in touch with an old friend recently, today's ideal for reaching out. Late-night inspiration could reveal the right money-making opportunity.

Monday 9th

If there's someone you're interested in, make a connection with them today. Send a text or invitation and use the right words to grab their attention. Your relationships prosper when you keep the lines of communication open. Find time to catch up with the one you love.

Tuesday 10th

If you feel downhearted first thing, make a point of writing things down to release unwanted emotions. There may be an upset regarding a friend, or perhaps you sense that your significant other wants to back off rather than get closer. Work could be a welcome diversion.

Wednesday 11th

It's a great date to get organised and sort things out at work and home. Make a list and aim for efficiency and order. You're on the verge of a significant turning point and may already sense that things are starting to shift and change, moving you in the right direction.

Thursday 12th

Your planet, Mars, turns direct today after ten weeks in retrograde. Think back to what you started in September 2022, as there may be a chance to try again or reawaken interest in your ideas and plans. Aim to sort out any miscommunication or misunderstandings that have taken place.

Friday 13th

It's an ideal date to flex your people skills and sort out a recent misunderstanding, perhaps with a sibling or neighbour. Be humble if necessary, or ask for forgiveness. Don't lose sight of your big dreams; visualise your chosen goal and draw up a vision board this weekend.

Saturday 14th

Today's stars have a feel-good vibe. It's a wonderful day for a first date or enjoying a love relationship. A friend may open up and reveal their true feelings. Make time for socialising and hang out with your favourite group of people. A women's group would be ideal.

Sunday 15th

Be wary of giving in too easily to another person's wants or needs. You may be tempted to try to buy someone's affections, but this isn't wise. Avoid lending money, and don't mix finance and friendship. It could be helpful to remember that you can't please everyone, even if you try.

Monday 16th

Taboo issues could crop up today, so be prepared to dive deep into some uncomfortable areas. If you're typical of your star sign, there may be a side to your nature that likes to walk on the wild side. Pay close attention both to your needs and those of your partner.

Tuesday 17th

The effort you put in is closely related to the rewards you receive. This isn't always true in life, but it's worth working hard now, especially if you're striving to meet a financial goal. Your sense of adventure could be awakened this evening. Say yes to a new experience.

Wednesday 18th

Keep your ears close to the ground as Mercury turns direct in your career zone. Something you hear could open a door and lead to a new job, role or position. Stepping into your power may require extra courage and determination. Be bold if an opportunity comes your way.

Thursday 19th

There could be a shift in personnel, or a job may come to an end. There's a theme of turning points in your life, of leaving one path behind and forging ahead down a new one. If this offers you more freedom or a friendlier work environment, you're on the right track.

Friday 20th

There's a shift in planetary energy from today onwards, as the Sun enters air sign Aquarius. This could be a welcome change from being over-worked or under pressure to find that you have more space and freedom. Make a firm decision over breakfast about what to do next.

Saturday 21st

Today's new moon takes place in Aquarius, and is linked to friend, group activities and wider society. It's these areas of life where you can set your intentions regarding your hopes and wishes, and get things moving. Join an online group or use social media to get your message across.

Sunday 22nd

If your money situation changes suddenly, view this as a sign to rework your strategy and consider your long-term goals. Your most important task now is to take a close look at your life and decide where you're heading and why. When it comes to love, promise commitment.

Monday 23rd

Lean on your friend this week and plan your next big adventure. Be clear about your boundaries within a love relationship or friendship. It might be time to redefine a "friend with benefits" liaison. Take some time out this evening to be quiet and listen to your inner voice.

Tuesday 24th

Look out for the friend who needs you. Your intervention could be a godsend to them, and you may enjoy taking on a protective role or practising generosity. If you're the one who's seeking help or support, reach out to others and ask for advice or assistance.

Wednesday 25th

It's an ideal day to practise prayer or meditation, even for a short while. This can help if you're currently seeking reassurance or guidance. Sometimes, you need to surrender to life as it is and admit when you're not in control. Your confidence could gain a welcome boost this evening.

Thursday 26th

The moon is in your star sign all day long, so focus on your needs. If you're feeling out of sorts, recognise what gives you comfort and helps to nurture and nourish your spirit. Listen to your dreams and notice life's signs or messages. What this shows could be a revelation.

Friday 27th

Being around a partner or friend with strong beliefs could rub off on you. Notice who comes into your life today, as this person may play a more significant role over the next couple of years than you might imagine. Actively seek beauty in the world in whatever form appeals.

Saturday 28th

Gifts and treats are on the cards today. You may be the one who's treating someone special, or perhaps you're the lucky recipient of a kind offer or gesture. Arts or crafts could turn into a money-making venture. Flex your creative muscle and see what materialises.

Sunday 29th

Doing things traditionally or conventionally doesn't fit your current astrology. You might consider changing your current career or job situation so you can work more from home or follow an unconventional work path. Follow your instincts today as they are unusually strong.

Monday 30th

This is an excellent week to send off an application and plan ahead. Look at ways you can revolutionise your financial situation, as a burst of inspiration could trigger a brainwave. Today's stars are great for spontaneity and right-brain thinking. Be innovative and alternative.

Tuesday 31st

You're an independent character, but don't go it alone. You need support, and would benefit from being around like-minded people for advice and inspiration. You may enjoy writing, or perfecting your sports skills. Anything that requires good hand-eye coordination ticks the box.

FEBRUARY

· · · · · · · · · · · · · · · · · ·

Wednesday 1st

Today's stars highlight intellectual freedom. Engage in group activities and discuss new ideas, especially those that impact society in general. Avoid in-depth work, especially if it's repetitive. You may be voting for a new boss at work. Prioritise family later on or plan a cosy evening at home.

Thursday 2nd

You'll be happiest today within your family or spending time at home – a DIY session, perhaps. If that's not possible, reach out to the ones you love and arrange a lunchtime meet-up. If you're harbouring romantic feelings, it's a good day to make a connection and let that person know.

Friday 3rd

You might be wearing different hats today, trying to keep up with work commitments as well as dealing with home or family business. Something's got to give, so decide where your priorities lie. It's a lovely evening for chilling out and relaxing. Watch a movie and have wine and popcorn to hand.

Saturday 4th

It may be difficult to switch off from work, but it's important to do so. Deal with anything urgent first thing so you can then turn your attention towards fun activities. It would be a great day to hang out with your children, go on a first date or take in some entertainment.

Sunday 5th

The less said in affairs of the heart, the better. Don't get caught up in a situation where you want to have the last word; instead, let it go. Today's full moon heightens emotions and your passionate nature might be on show. Love is at the forefront and there could be cause for celebration.

Monday 6th

You might have a case of the Monday morning blues and take a while to get going. Actively engage with creative ideas at work or at home, and throw yourself into a new project, as anything that uses visualisation or images to make an impact could go extraordinarily well.

Tuesday 7th

If you're true to your star sign, you have an argumentative nature. Be careful at work today as this side of your Aries temperament could kick in. You might be playing devil's advocate, but be wary of using words to hurt or wound others. Take your time before speaking out.

Wednesday 8th

You may be seeking advice if you have some concerns about a work or health issue. Reach out to the right person and they can quickly soothe your worries. It's worth investing in expert advice. You might lose yourself in a project or task, but the result should be worth it.

Thursday 9th

You could be buzzing with great ideas or be keen to talk to the boss or a person of influence. Leap into action first thing and grab your moment if this is true for you. Get on the right side of other people to smooth your progress – hone your people skills.

Friday 10th

There's a finality about your work or career. Something needs to be said or done so you can get it out of the way. You're moving into a new era or chapter next month, and you'll want to wrap things up before then. Don't give up; keep going and tick a major item off your to-do list.

Saturday 11th

If you're still focused on work, you might feel the tug between opposing priorities and a romantic relationship could get caught in the middle. However, your friends are another story, especially when there's no drama and it's easy to be with one another. Say yes to a group activity.

Sunday 12th

Uncomfortable emotions could arise today, especially if you start comparing yourself to other people and what you do and don't have. Money could be the trigger as you might get a financial wake-up call. Rather than acting impulsively, use this opportunity to reassess your values.

Monday 13th

It's a good day to take a closer look at what money means to you, as this area of your life is getting a shake-up thanks to unpredictable Uranus in your money zone. Be honest with yourself if things aren't working out the way you want them to.

Tuesday 14th

It's not the most romantic Valentine's Day, but it does look as if you could enjoy yourself. Admittedly, you might have your eye on an adventure and new experiences rather than love and romance. Whoever you're with today, be around those people who lift your spirits.

Wednesday 15th

Today's astrology is about spirituality for you, your religion or philosophy. You may be seeking meaning beyond the everyday, and need something to believe in that gives you hope and faith. The materialistic side of life could have less appeal or bring you less fulfilment.

Thursday 16th

An older friend could take on a significant role in your life. You might be handing over responsibility or asking for advice, or perhaps they require your help and you want to be there for them and repay their wisdom or kindness. Make time for the people you care about.

Friday 17th

It might be the last day of the working week, but it's not a day to slack off. You could work super-fast or take on an extra commitment that brings in some welcome cash. When you find a deeper purpose for your career or vocation, your work takes on new meaning.

Saturday 18th

The Sun's move into Pisces turns your attention inwards to your inner voice. You might really need to slow down because you feel tired or worried about a personal issue. If this is true for you, calm your mind and prioritise rest and relaxation.

Sunday 19th

If something's bothering you, find time to talk about it. Reach out to a good friend rather than keeping your feelings bottled up. Chill out, take it easy and don't try to do too much. Sometimes, you're wise to hand over a worry or concern and let life step in to guide you.

Monday 20th

Today's new moon falls in Pisces, which is a time to surrender and let go. This can feel disorienting for you as you like to be in charge. Sometimes, however, you have to lose yourself to find out who you are. Love is one area where losing yourself could be a complete joy.

Tuesday 21st

Listen to your dreams as they could help guide you. Lean into your spiritual side and dive deep into your beliefs, as this could be a source of comfort for you. Avoid a friend or group when your values are at odds, and remove yourself from a tricky situation.

Wednesday 22nd

You have the two best planets, Venus and Jupiter, in conjunction in Aries for the next few weeks. Make the most of it by trusting your luck, and be open to good fortune. Make time to reassess what you need or want in life and ask for guidance. A night spent with good friends is a welcome tonic.

Thursday 23rd

The more authentic you are and the more you stay true to your beliefs, the more likely you are to find contentment. Try not to be someone you're not but actively enjoy being the person you are. What you say or write could impact other people's lives in a good way.

Friday 24th

When it comes to your work, you may be gearing up to move away from a conventional path and try something alternative. This will require vision, a willingness to take a risk and a strong belief in what you're doing. Ensure you divide your attention equally between all three.

. . . .

Saturday 25th

Money matters are under the cosmic spotlight, so finances may require a new attitude or outlook. Change happens when you are controversial, exploring and inventive. You may experience a strong desire to bend or break the rules. Intellect is more important than feelings.

Sunday 26th

Have faith in what you're doing and don't let other people's opinions stop you in your tracks. It would be easy to give up now or believe what you hear, but see this as a challenge rather than a failure. Writing in a journal or speaking positive affirmations could strengthen your purpose.

Monday 27th

You have luck on your side, so do whatever's necessary to boost your confidence and make the most of your potential and good fortune. Whether you want love or money (or both!), take a calculated risk and go for it. Make "nothing ventured, nothing gained" today's motto.

Tuesday 28th

It's normal to have some level of fear or worry if you're stepping out of your comfort zone and trying something new. Don't let your worries hold you back. Instead, breathe deeply into your feelings and aim to transform fear into excitement. Rope your friends into helping out.

MARCH

Wednesday 1st

Remind yourself of life's simple pleasures, put self-care high on your list of priorities and savour life fully. You may not know where you're going to end up, but does it matter? At least aim to enjoy the ride. Start the new month slowly and take one step at a time.

Thursday 2nd

This is a brilliant day for activities that make you feel good. Engage in any area of your life that pleases you. New opportunities could take you away from your daily routine and are worth following up on. Love, too, could be magnificent. The stars are shining down on you!

Friday 3rd

Your emotions could feel intense in readiness for the full moon in a few days. Wherever life presents you with a challenge, look inside yourself for answers. You may be done with a situation at work or home. If so, take some time out rather than act impulsively.

Saturday 4th

The perfect antidote to stress is to unwind, let your hair down and have a good time. Engage only in those activities that bring you pleasure, and view the glass of life as half full. Enjoy yourself with your children, melt into a love affair, or simply sit quietly and witness nature's beauty.

Sunday 5th

Aries is one of the fire signs, so you tend to enjoy life most when you feel motivated and can act spontaneously. Bear this in mind now and make a concerted effort to look on the bright side of life. Smile when you meet new people, and be engaging, open and curious.

Monday 6th

During the full moon phase, you're looking at what you can complete or let go of in life rather than be thinking too much about what next. The focus may be on your health and wellbeing, and looking after yourself better. You might be stepping into a caring role.

Tuesday 7th

Saturn's move into Pisces lights up the sector of your horoscope that rules retreat and solitude. You might consciously take a step back from public life or decide to choose a path of service. Create space for solitude in your life and don't be afraid of saying no.

Wednesday 8th

Don't overload your schedule as you'll be more satisfied when you complete what you start. You may need time to yourself and realise that decluttering your surroundings brings inner clarity. If you want to start a detox or tweak your routine, you couldn't choose a better time.

Thursday 9th

You have an independent nature, but this isn't the time to go it alone. If you're in a relationship, reach out to the one you love and enjoy some quality time together. The more optimistic and upbeat you are, the more this rubs off on the people closest to you.

Friday 10th

Make time for connections, networking and communication. When you open up to other people, this often generates new ideas or useful information. Try not to rush through life, but instead stop and say hello to the people you meet every day. Take an interest in them.

Saturday 11th

You're a social person, so you thrive when you have good people in your life and you're on a mission. Flex your caring gene and reach out to help a person in need. Take the initiative when it comes to love, as a conversation that begins naturally could quickly turn romantic.

Sunday 12th

There's an emotional vibe today, which isn't always comfortable for you. Don't be scared of experiencing all your feelings; be vulnerable and open your heart to others. This could be a romantic time, or perhaps you find fulfilment helping out with a good cause.

Monday 13th

The Monday morning blues could kick in first thing, and you
may feel tired or down in the dumps. Allow yourself plenty
of time to get where you need to be as it won't feel great
turning up late. Make a point of seeking inspiration through
knowledge or education.

Tuesday 14th

You may feel unsteady or unsure of yourself. When you
feel vulnerable, it's sometimes easy to believe you're wrong
and another person is right, but don't be fooled or believe
everything you hear. Take your time, raise your vibe and don't
feel you have to rush into anything.

Wednesday 15th

This is a tricky phase for you if you feel insecure or you're
lacking confidence. Sometimes it only takes one small thing
not working out for you to have a wobble. Alternatively,
perhaps you're dealing with a significant personal issue. Either
way, be kind to yourself first and foremost.

Thursday 16th

In a few days, the Sun will light up Aries, your star sign. If
you're struggling, know that this is a symbol of light and hope.
Let go of whatever's not working and stay faithful. Venus'
move into your money zone is a reminder to get practical about
money and security.

Friday 17th

You don't need to rush into anything new at the moment. Instead, take your time and consider your long-term goals. This is especially important regarding your financial and emotional wellbeing. The conversation you have with yourself is the most important conversation you'll have today.

Saturday 18th

A problem shared is a problem halved. If you have an issue at work or in your personal life, turn to a good friend for help or advice. A social event could cost more than you expect but should be worth it when you have a good time. Say yes to a party or birthday celebration.

Sunday 19th

Talk planet Mercury enters your star sign today and you may be more than ready to speak up. It's a good time to reach out to other people and open up about your personal experiences. This may have a dual purpose of benefiting both you and the other person.

Monday 20th

It's your turn in the spotlight, as the Sun enters your star sign on the day of the equinox. The Sun represents vitality and energy, and turns the focus on you, your personal goals and aims, your body and your self-image. Boost your wellbeing and confidence in any way that suits you.

Tuesday 21st

Aries is the first sign of the zodiac, which means you're a pioneer and innovator. You're at your best when you're starting something new. The lure of a fresh start or a new challenge awakens you and today's new moon is the perfect time to consider what's coming up next.

Wednesday 22nd

You're likely to feel focused and motivated under the gaze of the new moon. It's a good time to get ahead and you can be the first off the starting block. If you have new ideas bubbling away, write them down and say them out loud to send them out into the universe.

Thursday 23rd

This is a transitional phase. You might be ready to close the door on the past when a job ends, or you might step down from a position of leadership. If someone's absent from your life or has taken a step back, let them. This isn't the time to rush in to help.

Friday 24th

This week's astrology is primarily about putting yourself and your own needs first. Love could be a great comfort. Snuggle up with the ones you love, which includes your pets. When it comes to money, expect some ups and downs. Act fast and you could grab yourself a bargain.

Saturday 25th

You're likely to be busier at home or within your family over the next few weeks. You might be starting building work or be keen to renovate the place you live. Be more proactive and engaged in family affairs. If you need to intervene in someone else's life, go for it.

Sunday 26th

There may be something you want to say but you're finding it hard to do so, or maybe you can't find the right words. 11:11 is a special number, so this may be a good time to speak up or share your thoughts and ideas. Be confident in your voice and speak with authority.

Monday 27th

It's a lively beginning to the new week, so start as you mean to go on. You could get a lot done in record time. Plus, when you open up to others and ask for what you want or need, it encourages magic to happen. A gift of help, insight or inspiration is the reward.

Tuesday 28th

Today's stars are potentially lucky, and a lovely date for vision work or considering your long-term goals and aims. It's a great week for stretching your comfort zone. You may hear some news that's delightful or boosts your spirits. The more you put into life, the more you get back!

Wednesday 29th

Turn your attention to money matters, especially concerning your home and family. Get on top of your financial goals and look at how you can work alongside other people to boost your resources. Only offer your money if it's a gift rather than a loan.

Thursday 30th

This is a time of change for you, especially when it comes to money and finances, and it can go either way. Perhaps you will receive a gift or lucky break, or maybe you need to rethink the way you spend or earn money. This could affect someone close if you're in a relationship or married.

Friday 31st

There are times in life when you need to realise that it's okay to be self-motivated or self-oriented. You can't always save or help other people, however much you want to. Put your own needs first and see this as an act of ultimate kindness to yourself.

APRIL

Saturday 1st

Be wary of going on a shopping binge today, as you might find yourself spending way more than you intend to. Ideally, find cheap or free ways of enjoying yourself – once you start contemplating what's possible, you may be pleasantly surprised. Luck strikes at lunch or in the early afternoon.

Sunday 2nd

It's worth getting up early to spend time with someone dear to your heart. Have a sociable breakfast and enjoy putting the world to rights. You may not be in the mood to get organised or prioritise your health later on. Get a family member to help you.

Monday 3rd

It's a good week to be bold when it comes to money and to do whatever you can to earn more or shore up your reserves. If you're doing well financially, this is not the time to let things slip or be slap-dash when it comes to money. Don't promise more than you can afford.

Tuesday 4th

Keep close tabs on work and money, and don't let any fears or worries kick in. Adopt a positive approach to career and finances. Focus on what is working out rather than giving too much energy to what isn't. Act fast, be decisive, keep moving forward.

Wednesday 5th

A sensible approach to finances is recommended. Look to the long-term future and set up a savings plan or deal with debt. Keep a close eye on what's happening in the world of economics and plan your strategy accordingly. If you're in a relationship or married, work as a team.

Thursday 6th

The spotlight's on your one-to-ones during today's full moon. It may be a peak time for love, or perhaps tempers flare and you'll need to clear the air. Aim for honesty and fairness in your relationships. It's a good date to make a decision, as long as you consider both sides of the coin.

Friday 7th

Your best strategy today is to be creative and come up with new ideas for earning or financial security. Love is a key feature as it may be that your partner's success rubs off on you. Prioritise your family or loved ones over this Easter weekend.

Saturday 8th

Being with your family could be helpful in more ways than one. This is a promising time to pool resources and ideas about money and security. It's important that you walk your talk and set a good example, especially for someone younger. Don't overestimate what's possible.

Sunday 9th

It could be easy this morning to get caught up with serious issues that leave you no time for fun. Yes, it's important to sort things out with a loved one and deal with any personal issues, but all work and no play won't lift your spirits. Make time for both.

Monday 10th

It's an ideal date for a road trip or to go somewhere you've never been before. This is particularly important if you've spent the last few days at home or with your family. Encourage the ones you love to join you on your adventure, or strike out on your own.

Tuesday 11th

This is one of the luckiest days of the year for you. If ever there was a time to put your needs first, it's now. As an Aries, you get easily bored so reach out and start something new. Broaden your horizons, say yes to life, take a risk, embrace freedom.

Wednesday 12th

It may be hard to pull yourself away from your family or home, but you're wise to do so. Even if you're missing out, now's the time to turn your attention towards work and money. Find a shortcut or try a new initiative to speed up your job or chores.

Thursday 13th

Find a deeper purpose for your work or money-making activities, which may include taking care of loved ones. Sometimes it can be hard to knuckle down and get the job done, especially if you sense that you're the one who needs to step up and take on the responsibility.

Friday 14th

There's a weekend vibe as soon as the day begins, with a focus on socialising. You might be keen to get work or chores out of the way so you can meet up with friends. Not everything may go according to plan this evening. Be a shoulder to lean on if necessary.

Saturday 15th

You may find it challenging to be with a group of people if you have conflicting values. Try not to let this spoil your enjoyment and agree to keep your differences aside. The day is likely to get better as it goes on, especially when you meet up with people of like minds.

Sunday 16th

If you've not had a day to yourself recently or you've been super busy, chill out, relax and do very little. You could start off feeling lonely or think you're missing out, but see this as a chance to recharge your batteries. Be with family or loved ones later on.

Monday 17th

You'll do yourself a favour by easing your way into the working week. If you can start the week slowly and prioritise activities that benefit you and boost your wellbeing, so much the better.

Tuesday 18th

You're back in the driving seat today – as long as you've ensured that your needs are met. When you're fully nourished and nurtured, your energy often reappears as if by magic. Try not to get grumpy if home or family demands take up your time this evening.

Wednesday 19th

You may not want to deal with the serious side of life today, but don't ignore what's going on. It can be an uplifting experience to embrace your freedom as long as you don't get carried away. Keep your feet on the ground and take practical steps to sort things out.

Thursday 20th

Today's solar eclipse signifies a major turning point. This is about a deep and powerful transformation for you, possibly involving your personal goals and wellbeing, or a makeover. Either way, it's potentially an exciting new beginning that could emerge from an emotional time.

Friday 21st

Know that money is an emotional trigger and be careful not to over-spend. This is not the time for splurging; instead, keep an eye on your spending habits. Play a waiting game if necessary and work out a plan to save for the things you want.

Saturday 22nd

If money is a problem right now, reach out to other people for advice and ideas. Approach someone in a position of influence and ask for their help. This might be your boss or someone who can offer financial guidance. Be honest about what's going on for you.

Sunday 23rd

It's a great day to meet up with a sibling or relative. Alternatively, join your partner and meet up with someone who means a lot to them. If you're on your own, find someone to talk to or pop round to the neighbours'. A community venture could provide the joy you're seeking.

Monday 24th

It's worth going over old ground and readdressing a personal issue. This may be to do with finances, your family or a property move. An agreement that was made early in the month could require a new approach or fresh input. View this as the planning stage.

Tuesday 25th

Home and family affairs are under the cosmic spotlight. It's here where new beginnings are likely, whether you're making an independent move or welcoming a new addition to the family. It's a lovely day to reminisce or spend time with an older member of your family.

Wednesday 26th

There may be more than one reason why you're meeting up with family this week. Someone might require your financial or emotional assistance, or perhaps you're the one asking for help. If you enjoy being with your family, that may be reason enough to get together.

Thursday 27th

If you're a parent, keep an eye on a child's spending or money habits. If you sense they're struggling financially or spending more than they can afford, make a point of intervening. It may not be a popular move but it could serve you both well in the long run.

Friday 28th

Be innovative when it comes to money. You could find a clever way to cut your losses or expenses or come up with a genius idea to revolutionise your cash situation. What you must do is engage with what's going on; don't create a potential crisis by ignoring the signs.

Saturday 29th

The play zone of your horoscope teams up nicely with the weekend. Put work and money matters to one side and get on with the serious business of enjoying yourself. Have fun with your kids, line up a romantic date or organise a social get-together. Be decisive and direct.

Sunday 30th

If you feel any area of your life is out of control, today might be a good time to get back on top of things and take charge. You may want to focus on fitness and health, or have a mega day sorting and tidying. Clear the decks in readiness for the new month.

MAY

Monday 1st

Bank Holiday Monday could coincide with some money magic. Revisit your previous ideas, look again at your financial plans, or ensure your life admin is all up to date. An eclipse in your money zone at the end of the week could prove pivotal. Forewarned is forearmed.

Tuesday 2nd

If you're in a relationship or married, carve out some time in your diary for a deep and meaningful encounter. If you're looking for love, meet up with an old friend as this could act as a stepping stone to a romantic introduction. Past connections may prove useful in more ways than one.

Wednesday 3rd

There's no guarantee that you will get on with your in-laws. If you have a tricky time dealing with your partner's loved ones, it's best not to get involved with them today. Tempers could flare, especially if you don't see eye-to-eye.

Thursday 4th

You might find it hard to make sense of your thoughts or speak eloquently today. Chopping and changing your mind could drive you nuts. However, when you shift your mindset or think outside of the box, this can help you resolve an ongoing personal problem or issue.

Friday 5th

Today's lunar eclipse lights up the money zones of your horoscope. Keep your options open and don't reveal everything. At the same time, it's important not to ignore any warning signs which crop up. If you already know that your financial situation is changing, make a plan for the future.

Saturday 6th

During this eclipse period, it's important to note that you're not on your own. Reaching out to other people can bring you comfort and security. You might find that loved ones are on your wavelength and by your side. Be there for one another and offer emotional support.

Sunday 7th

The planet Venus brings some much-needed peace and harmony to your home and family zone. If things have been tempestuous of late or your home life has been noisy for whatever reason, you're moving into a gentler, calmer period. And breathe…

Monday 8th

You'll want more than the everyday and mundane now. Try to find a way to expand your horizons or line up something to look forward to. Mercury retrograde in your money zone isn't the best time to spend big, but don't let that stop you from exploring all your options.

Tuesday 9th

Money remains a potentially tricky area of your life. This could be because of a shift in earnings or your current financial situation. You might be paying out, perhaps on technology, but try to look at new ways of earning or getting on top of your life admin.

Wednesday 10th

You may find it easier to concentrate at work today, so focus on the job at hand. Your family may prove distracting, but providing for your loved ones can bring a true sense of fulfilment into your life (even if you do fall out now and again).

Thursday 11th

If you've fallen out with a friend, or there's someone in your life you haven't seen for a long time, those painful emotions could reappear this morning. Try not to be disheartened if this is true for you, and don't feel that you have to be on your own. Reach out.

Friday 12th

It's potentially a good day to do your sums or balance the books. Admittedly, there may be more money going out than coming in right now, but that may hopefully shift and change before too long. For now, be realistic and practical about what you can and can't afford.

Saturday 13th

A third party could intervene today and help you out of a tricky spot. Be open to this person's ideas and potentially willing to let them step in and take charge. If you need a break or some time alone, you could decide to cancel a social engagement. Do whatever's right for you.

Sunday 14th

Slow things down today and ensure you have a lazy Sunday. If you're seeking answers, find somewhere quiet and turn your focus within for guidance. If you're struggling, hold tight to the knowledge that tomorrow is another day.

Monday 15th

Turning points abound in this new week. Firstly, communication planet Mercury turns direct in your money zone. You may receive the news you've been waiting for, or the payment that's been delayed. Reach out and communicate confidently about money matters.

Tuesday 16th

Yesterday's stars brought change, but today's stars bring a major turning point your way which could potentially be full of abundance. When you have the best planet in your money zone, you're right to be open to good fortune and practise the law of attraction.

Wednesday 17th

Trust your instincts around money. You may receive a gift or bonus out of the blue, or you may be ambitious to earn more. Dig deep to reveal your money motivations, especially as you have the best planet boosting your wealth zone for the next twelve months.

Thursday 18th

You would do well to be ruthless around money and stay on the right side of the law today. There's a sense of renewal, a chance to commit to a new path to transform your financial situation. Don't rely too heavily on other people but take charge of your finances.

Friday 19th

A radical move or reshuffle could create space for something new to emerge. Money is a key factor, so the main message of today's new moon is to consider what you can do differently if the sums don't add up. It's an opportunity to reset your money goals and acknowledge your self-worth.

Saturday 20th

Your planet, Mars, leaves behind an emotional water sign and enters a passionate fire sign today, which is great news for you. It may feel as though you're being reborn or re-energised. Commit to doing more of what you love and less wallowing in the future.

Sunday 21st

You could experience a power surge now, but be wary that it doesn't go to your head. Life may present you with an opportunity to see how you react when you don't get what you want. Keeping the lines of communication open could help you make sense of current events.

Monday 22nd

Start any communications that can help you resolve a financial issue. Donate to a food bank or share what you have with others. It's worth reaching out to resolve an argument that may have flared up over the weekend; there's more chance of reaching an agreement today.

Tuesday 23rd

You may be tempted to throw money at a problem, but it's not the best day to get carried away or make a grand gesture. Instead, reach out to others in a caring way. A hug or some kind words could be all that's needed to re-establish a bond.

Wednesday 24th

Tensions may rise first thing. Notice whether there's a person in your life who acts as a trigger, someone around whom you instantly feel pent up or irritated, and check whether there's any projection going on between you. This evening looks great for doing more of what you love.

Thursday 25th

Money matters could remain a source of frustration, but try not to let them stop you from enjoying yourself and making the most of life. Today is ideal for embracing the people and things you cherish. Focus on happy times and be around people who make you laugh and lift your spirits.

Friday 26th

Your feelings of motivation and excitement could continue to grow today. You may enjoy a spontaneous conversation with a neighbour, have a flirtatious encounter, or feel inspired when you hear new ideas. Feeding off a competitive situation could get you fired up in a good way.

Saturday 27th

You may not be in the mood for work or chores today, but once you throw yourself into an obligation or responsibility, you could start to enjoy yourself. If whatever you're involved in brings in some extra cash, even better. Prioritise your health.

Sunday 28th

Life might step in to slow you down. If you're trying to do too much, pick one task and complete it. If you're typical of your star sign, you love the lure of the new but don't always find it easy to finish what you start. Someone close may need a shoulder to lean on.

Monday 29th

You may experience some confusion first thing or find it a challenge to tackle anything practical. Take your time and know that you'll get going as the day progresses. Teamwork could make any Bank Holiday activity more enjoyable, and you'll get the job done.

Tuesday 30th

Today is all about your close relationships. The more in sync you are with other people, the smoother and easier your progress. Ask for support or advice at work and find the person who complements your skills. Make time for romance and be with the ones you love.

Wednesday 31st

You may be a little more protective with your emotions today. You might prefer to stick to what's familiar rather than venture out with your heart on your sleeve. When it comes to family and domestic matters, you may need to help a partner iron out a personal issue.

JUNE

Thursday 1st
Keep your money in your pocket first thing. You could be tempted to make a spontaneous purchase to cheer yourself up, but you're wise not to rush in. This afternoon is great for research and any task that requires intense focus. Work on a long-term idea or plan.

Friday 2nd
You may be gearing up to make an investment. If this is linked to travel or study, you're on the right track. You may be in the mood to spend first and work out how to pay for it later, but it's important to work out if you can afford what you want to do. Have a romantic night in.

Saturday 3rd
It's a full moon weekend and emotions could be heightened. If you're jetting off somewhere exotic, you're in tune with your stars. Your desire for adventure and new experiences is being awakened. Alternatively, it's a great weekend to attend a study course or workshop.

Sunday 4th
The full moon lights up your education zone and you might want more from life than the everyday or mundane. You could be willing to spend money to invest in your education or gain new qualifications. When it comes to making money, think outside of the box.

Monday 5th

Love planet Venus moves into your romance zone today, where it will remain for an unusually long time. This is likely to be an intriguing period for your love life, but it could start with an ending rather than a new beginning. Reassess what you want when it comes to relationships.

Tuesday 6th

You're not easily satisfied if your work is routine and you're doing the same job day in, day out. Today mostly requires a slow and steady approach, yet there may also be room for innovation and doing things differently. Bring something new to the mix and share your ideas with your boss.

Wednesday 7th

Your emotions may be running on turbo speed today. There's intensity in the air and passion in the breeze. If you want an easy life, you shouldn't return to an ex or reignite an illicit love affair, however much you're tempted. Do the right thing in your romantic liaisons.

Thursday 8th

When you have both Venus and Mars, the "lovers of the heavens", in your romance zone, you know this is likely to be a hot and passionate time for love. You might enjoy the chase, even if a new connection doesn't develop into a relationship.

Friday 9th

Slow things down today and take a step back. You may need some time on your own, or perhaps you want time out from a relationship to catch your breath and think things through. It's a good time to establish new rules and boundaries about what's okay and what's not.

Saturday 10th

It's a good weekend to get back to basics and notice what brings you solace and comfort. If you're out of sorts and life's been busy, you may decide to cancel a social engagement and catch up on your rest instead. It could also help to keep your cash in your pocket.

Sunday 11th

Today's stars flag up an issue with a parent or authority figure. You may return to a situation in your life that requires your attention. Going back to a job or previous role could be a good move financially. Ensure you ask all the right questions before leaping in.

Monday 12th

If you're in tune with your stars, you may be fired up and raring to go today, feeling refreshed and recharged after the weekend. Your competitive nature could kick in too, and you might feel more able to look on the bright side of life and focus on what's good in your life.

Tuesday 13th

You'll be at your best around other people today, and part of a diverse and lively social scene. Play around with new ideas, find out new information, and generally stay busy and active. The only downside is that you may need to come to terms with recent changes at work.

Wednesday 14th

If you have no financial responsibility other than looking after yourself, today could feel abundant. You may see where a new income stream might come from, or perhaps you might receive a gift. If you have children or you're in a relationship, you're more likely to notice where money's going out.

Thursday 15th

Stay engaged with money matters, especially if you're seeking ways to earn more. This area of your life is where there's likely to be change and more ups and downs than usual. Ensure your CV is up to date if you're applying for work, or stay informed on financial trends by checking the news.

Friday 16th

There may be something you're not able to say at the moment, whether you're the one holding back or you're keeping someone's secret. Alternatively, you might be aware of where your knowledge or experience is lacking. For now, think things through without taking action.

Saturday 17th

There's a shift in pace today. You might benefit from some time out to think about where you're heading and why. If one path led you nowhere, stop and reconsider what to do next. When it comes to love, it's an ideal date for a heart-to-heart. Keep things friendly and light.

Sunday 18th

Today's new moon falls in your communication zone. Be around other people, as you'll feel happier when you have friends to chat to and things going on socially. Gemini rules your local community, and you may find yourself wanting to pitch in and get involved during this phase.

Monday 19th

Get ahead with admin, applications, paperwork and bureaucracy today, as the new moon energy is forward-moving. You could take on a lot and find a way to get most of it done. If you're a typical Aries, you are more efficient when you're busy.

Tuesday 20th

Make a decisive move regarding finances and security. Find the right leader or influencer to follow and the results could be worth it. It's a good time to invest in expert advice, especially concerning a financial or legal situation. Get things sorted out at home or within your family.

Wednesday 21st

Today marks the solstice. For you, this turns your attention towards your home and family, your past and where you come from. You may be returning to your childhood home. Alternatively, you could be talking to a child about their heritage and legacy.

Thursday 22nd

It's a wonderful day for romance and being with the one you love. This could be a child, or someone you adore deeply. You might be heading off on a first date or be back in touch with someone you loved previously. You could even spend over the odds to treat someone special.

Friday 23rd

Pay attention to the basics of life now. Ensure you eat well, get some exercise and take good care of your wellbeing. You don't need anything fancy or extravagant today. Simple pleasures should be enough and could bring a strong sense of contentment and fulfilment.

Saturday 24th

You may choose to work today, especially if you're paid well. It's a good day to ensure that things are in order in your life. Have a tidying day, sort out admin or paperwork, do the cleaning or catch up on your accounts. Enjoy completing routine tasks.

Sunday 25th

You may want more peace and quiet in your life. Any kind of spiritual practice would help, especially if you've experienced significant changes over the last couple of months. Take a few minutes out to reflect and breathe, and turn your attention inwards.

Monday 26th

Tempers could flare today. There may be someone in your life who's behaving unacceptably, perhaps a lover, or a child who's out of control. It's not a good time to be impulsive with money and you're wise to rein in your daredevil nature. Take things slowly.

Tuesday 27th

Talk planet Mercury moves into Cancer today, pulling you back towards your past. If you're at home more during this time, be open and talk about your experiences. Find ways to reconnect with family and loved ones. It would be a wonderful day to be introduced to a partner's family.

Wednesday 28th

Spend the next few days dealing with practicalities. Take even one small step towards sorting out a financial issue and you'll feel a strong sense of relief. This may be linked to your familial relationships. Whatever you've been avoiding, now's the time to tackle it head-on.

Thursday 29th

Consider your future and long-term plans, especially when it comes to your home and property, your family and your legacy. You may be helping out with a parent or be taking on a more adult role within your family. If in doubt, choose the sensible option and do what's right.

Friday 30th

It could be a wonderful day for a family get-together. Firm up some plans for a future celebration or anniversary, or decide where you're going on holiday as a group. Create some time and space to listen to your intuition and pay close attention to your dreams.

JULY

Saturday 1st

It's a lovely day for visiting family or returning to a place that holds many happy memories. There's a feel-good vibe about your stars, and you could receive a gift or new opportunity that restores your confidence. It's a lucky day for property matters.

Sunday 2nd

It's worth taking a trip today to meet up with someone special in your life. You might be visiting a child or relative, a lover or a good friend. Try not to raise your expectations too high if you're on a romantic quest, as your lover may behave erratically.

Monday 3rd

During today's full moon, it's important to be realistic about your job options and aim to work hard to achieve your goals. You might have to make a big decision over whether to commit to a work project or stop what you're doing so you can spend more time at home.

Tuesday 4th

Set your sights on the next six months to the end of the year. A job or work situation may be proving a challenge, or perhaps it's not what you want to be doing. Think of this period as a time of completion and wrapping things up ready for a new beginning.

Wednesday 5th

Widen your social circle and team up with other people at work. You may be less interested in a conventional job or corporate goal, and more interested in playing your part within society. Consider the charities you support, and align yourself with a group or organisation you respect.

Thursday 6th

You may get caught up in a friend's drama today, and it won't matter what you say because they have their fixed opinion about who's wrong and who's right. Now may not be the time to try to change their views; instead, aim to listen to their story without laying judgement.

Friday 7th

It's a good day to sort things out regarding your foundations and security. See what steps you can take to feel more grounded. It's a great time for reconciliation or a heart-to-heart with a family member. Make the right moves and this could free things up for you financially.

Saturday 8th

If you're a typical Aries, you'll want everything to happen immediately. However, today's stars are encouraging you to act less and ponder more. Having no plans for the weekend could leave you floundering, but if you stop and listen to your inner voice, new ideas might emerge.

Sunday 9th

You'll have more get up and go today, and might know exactly what you need to make you happy. Dive into an activity that you love, or work on your personal goals and aims. This evening, spend time with family or loved ones reminiscing about times gone by.

Monday 10th

Your planet, Mars, enters earth sign Virgo today, where it remains until late August. This highlights your work and health, lifestyle and routine. Use this period to complete work projects, get organised and respect the mind-body-spirit connection. You might consider dropping everything for a family member this evening.

Tuesday 11th

Mercury's change of star sign emphasises the importance of family and loved ones. The more you look on the bright side of life and tap into your fire sign optimism, the more in step you are with the universe sending out the right messages. Your flirtatious nature could kick in.

Wednesday 12th

You could experience a shift in earnings or a change in your financial situation. You might be paying out, perhaps on technology. Give love this week, but keep your money in your pocket unless it's a necessary investment that benefits you in the long run.

Thursday 13th

You could be everyone's super chatty best friend today. You might take great pleasure in your daily affairs and enjoy reading and learning more. You may not appreciate being tied to your desk, as you could be easily distracted.

Friday 14th

Listen to your heart: if you think of someone close, get in touch; if a particular place keeps appearing in your mind, go and visit. Begin to explore new opportunities and don't just stick with your tried-and-tested routines. Family and money are linked by a spontaneous act.

Saturday 15th

Make time for someone special this lunchtime. Line up a romantic date or catch up with a good friend. Home and family affairs are on the verge of moving into a new chapter. This might create more admin or paperwork, so you're wise to get on top of things this weekend.

Sunday 16th

The dark of the moon is traditionally a time for rest and retreat, so take time out if you can. Slowing down for a short while and being quiet can help you hear your inner voice. It's even more important to do so if you have some big decisions coming up.

Monday 17th

Today's new moon highlights your home and family sector. It's in these areas of your life where you may be setting new intentions or getting ready for a new beginning. It's important to keep hold of hope and faith.

Tuesday 18th

Home and family matters are under the cosmic spotlight. Even though it's a new moon, you might experience something coming to an end regarding these areas of your life. It's a good day to make a decision about your next steps, especially concerning a child, parent or living situation.

Wednesday 19th

Stay connected with loved ones and your family. Listen to your emotions when it comes to your personal life and act instinctively if someone needs your help or support. A conversation with a child could offer great insight. Make a wish when you first catch sight of the crescent moon.

Thursday 20th

Your personal life could be extra romantic or dreamy. You may be experiencing deep love for someone in your life, perhaps a child or partner. There may be some concerns about your work or health. It's here where you might need to dig a little deeper and be resourceful.

Friday 21st

Don your business hat today and get serious. "Where there's a will, there's a way" is a great motto for your current astrology. Knuckle down and get on with the job or tasks at hand. If what you're doing pays well, this could be the incentive you need. Prove your determination.

Saturday 22nd

A chapter in your personal life may be coming to an end. You might be saying goodbye to a loved one or be moving on from your home. The wheel of life turns constantly. Sometimes, new beginnings only arise when you're willing to let go of the past.

Sunday 23rd

The Sun's move into Leo today is good news for your creativity. You might be excited about a project you're working on, or perhaps your writer's block shifts overnight. Today's events could represent a turning point in your love life. You may recognise that you're not the one in control.

Monday 24th

This is a fertile period of learning and insight when it comes to what you want in relationships. You may begin to recognise that what you're doing isn't good for you. If this is true for you, think of this as a chance to press the reset button on what's not working out.

Tuesday 25th

Over the next six weeks, you may ponder what love means to you. You could be yearning for someone from your past, or your heart may slowly open to someone new – perhaps a new child or a beloved pet. Know that there's no rush, and savour your deep emotions.

Wednesday 26th

Today's astrology favours saving rather than spending, investing rather than drawing up debt. Turn your attention to work and money matters, and create the right environment so you can focus and concentrate. If you're a keen writer, this could be the time to pen your masterpiece.

Thursday 27th

You may be in a romantic situation where you can't have what you want. If this is true for you, don't block out your emotions but experience them fully. An encounter with someone you loved and lost could turn out to be truly heart-warming.

Friday 28th

Talk planet Mercury enters Virgo today. This offers you a chance to work efficiently and take charge of your life rather than feeling like life is running you. A strong work ethic pays off, and you're more likely to stick to a healthy eating plan or regular exercise routine.

Saturday 29th

The moon in your travel zone energises your desire to spread your wings and broaden your horizons, so it's a divine time to be off on your travels this weekend. Alternatively, you may be spending the weekend studying something new.

Sunday 30th

If you're not on holiday, you may be busy with your hobbies and skills. If there's a writer within you, this is the ideal time to journal and play around with words. Find your craft, your sport, your chosen activity; you might find you have the discipline to really refine your work today.

Monday 31st

It's a new week, an ideal opportunity to focus more on work and organisation than play and good times. Don't forget, though, that a happy work/life balance suits you best. Today's stars feel productive, so you could get a lot done, including boosting your bank balance.

AUGUST

Tuesday 1st

The full moon is traditionally a time of celebration. You may know a Leo friend with a birthday and be invited to attend their party. You might also be reassessing your friendships or advising a child to do the same. Work and money matters are on a roll.

Wednesday 2nd

You may be tired today if you were awake in the night. Try to write down any worries rather than keep them buried. It could be a productive time of year for you, but don't overdo it and take on too much. "All work and no play" isn't the Aries way.

Thursday 3rd

Switch off your phone and social media if you've got a deadline to meet or a project to finish. Some quiet time might help restore your energy levels and enable you to get your head down and stay focused. When it comes to your health, don't discount a second opinion.

Friday 4th

As much as you may want to rush to get a job or task completed, you must pay attention to the details – don't miss out a vital part of the process. Reacquaint yourself with the fable of the tortoise and the hare: more haste, less speed.

Saturday 5th

You have the moon in Aries for the whole weekend, so put yourself and your needs first. You may feel more in touch with your emotions but in a way that energises you and makes you very present in your life. A late-night party or social event may be a joyful occasion.

Sunday 6th

The feel-good vibes continue into Sunday. You'll be happiest when you prioritise what you want to do rather than trying to keep other people happy. You may be working on a personal project, or be keen to get ahead with a goal or aim that's important to you. Love steps in this evening.

Monday 7th

If the good times continued into yesterday evening, you may need to rally today to stay on top of your responsibilities. Keep focused on what you want to achieve at work or home. Be firm with other people and let them know you need to get on with few distractions.

Tuesday 8th

Make a money wish today and see what transpires. You currently have the entrepreneurial planets in your money zone so their influence is strong. You may reap your rewards for your recent hard work.

Wednesday 9th

If there's someone in your life who's behaving erratically, this person may dominate events again. If you're involved in an on-off love relationship, it's more likely to be off than on. A cosmic warning light might flash on if you hand over money without due care and forethought.

Thursday 10th

You may receive good news today concerning a course of study or gaining qualifications. If you're looking for work, it's an ideal date to apply for a job or rewrite your CV. Taking on some extra work could be beneficial financially. Ask for what you want or need.

Friday 11th

The social vibe kicks in again, which is great if you're off work but not so helpful if you've got a lot to do. Be realistic about what you can achieve. Notice when you're feeling guilty, perhaps around a sibling or neighbour. Don't get mad but be honest about what you're feeling.

Saturday 12th

It's an ideal day to hang out with your family or spend a quiet day at home. Be strict with yourself, however, and don't waste time on frivolous or meaningless activities. Switch off social media and be attentive to the people you're with. That includes when you spend time on your own.

Sunday 13th

If you're looking for love, think about giving a second chance to a relationship that didn't work out the first time around. This isn't about commitment or making a big relationship move; instead, it's about keeping things playful, examining your feelings closely and reassessing what you want.

Monday 14th

You may be feeling soulful first thing, or missing a member of your family. Actively engage with activities you love to quickly boost your spirits. Sunshine creates a feel-good vibe, as does hanging out with people who make you happy.

Tuesday 15th

You may decide you want to have more fun today, hanging out with your kids or doing whatever pleases you. If that's what you need, go for it. Fire signs like yourself are often happiest when they're fulfilling their needs. The party vibe continues after work and into the evening.

Wednesday 16th

Today's new moon is an ideal time to start something new, turn to a fresh page and say yes to life. Consider what you're birthing or bringing into the world. This could be a skill or talent, a baby or news of a pregnancy. Step up the pace and find your passion.

Thursday 17th

The cosmic vibe turns more serious today, urging you to pay close attention to your work and your health. If you've been burning the candle at both ends, it's a good day to catch up, take the pace slow and aim to lead a moderate lifestyle. It's not exciting, but it's a worthy goal.

Friday 18th

You could end the working week feeling proud of what you've achieved. Even if you didn't work hard every day, make amends now and throw yourself into work, chores or activity. Your brainpower is working well, so put your mind to good use.

Saturday 19th

If you're in a relationship or married, this is an ideal weekend to be together and enjoy some quality time. You may want to explore somewhere different, or you might be happy simply hanging out together at home or in the garden. Re-energise your one-to-one time.

Sunday 20th

The loving vibes continue today, whether you're falling in love or in a long-term relationship. Even if you're single, you could still experience a romantic encounter, perhaps later on this evening. Put yourself in the way of love and be open to whatever comes your way.

Monday 21st

Don't let work dominate today. If you have a difficult boss or you're in a challenging work situation, it may be hard to leave work on time. Be resolute and firm in your decisions. Don't put business before pleasure and drop out on a loved one.

Tuesday 22nd

It would be easy to go round in circles or lose yourself trying to work things out in your head. Alternatively, you might be chasing after a bigger purpose in life or seeking a sense of deeper meaning regarding your job or work situation. If you need to take a break, make it happen.

Wednesday 23rd

Virgo season is officially here, heralding order and organisation, but you may be slowed down by Mercury, which turns retrograde today. This three-week phase may be beneficial for exploration and research. Go back to someone you met previously, whether for a work or health matter.

Thursday 24th

Be wary of a tendency to overthink things. Instead, use Mars'
energy to be active: if you're a writer, write; if you want to get
fit, start jogging; if you want to change your diet, put plans in
place so you can make it happen. You could feel extraordinarily
powerful today!

Friday 25th

You may start the day feeling invincible, as though you're
in your power and nothing can stop you. You might choose
to channel your ambition and drive into your career and
vocational goals. Alternatively, you could be a white knight on
your steed, helping out other people.

Saturday 26th

The emphasis for the next few days is on work. This doesn't
necessarily mean you'll be busy with your regular job, but it
does suggest it's time for reassessment and considering where
you're heading and why. This is an important part of the
Mercury retrograde phase.

Sunday 27th

If your hard work ethic is wearing thin, it's time to take stock
and think about what's next for you. Turn your attention
towards the people in your life and aim for partnership in all
things. Ensure that your relationships are based on equality,
with even levels of give and take.

Monday 28th

Whatever you decided over the weekend, put those wheels in motion today. It may be a bold move on your part, but trust your intuition. People are important later in the day, so find those who can help, guide and advise you well. Equally, see if you can provide support to someone today.

Tuesday 29th

You might be on a rollercoaster ride regarding your work and earnings. That's not to say you can't win big now; changing direction completely could work in your favour. Be careful what you promise, though, and don't give away more money than you can afford.

Wednesday 30th

We're building towards the full moon, which could be an emotional time for you. You may feel disoriented and unsure where you're heading. Keep close tabs on how you're feeling to avoid falling back into bad habits.

Thursday 31st

The full moon's potential this week is spiritual, creative and compassionate, but perhaps tiring, too. Pace yourself, and if you need some time out, do less and be more. If you're more emotional than usual, allow yourself to let go of your feelings. Give in and surrender to life as it is.

SEPTEMBER

· · · · · · · · · · · · · · · · ·

Friday 1st

Pay close attention to your dreams, as your subconscious could be unusually revealing. Ease your way into the working day. You may experience an energy boost from lunchtime onwards. You're a hot-blooded individual, and the evening promises passionate romance and arguments.

Saturday 2nd

Be more yin than yang today, especially if you're spending time with the one you love. If you're typical of your star sign, you like to have things your way, but your relationships might flourish when you learn to give more than you receive. Be around people who make you happy.

Sunday 3rd

Try not to harbour resentments or pent-up emotions if there's someone in your life who's a major challenge. This might be a parent, authority figure or your boss. Aim to be more accepting of your situation, especially if you know that you're in it for the long run.

Monday 4th

Venus' change of direction indicates a turning point for your relationship with a lover or child. Today is potentially a lucky day for you, and money matters could improve. If you have to choose between money or love, follow your heart rather than your head.

Tuesday 5th

Turn your attention to life admin today. You might be paying bills or sorting out your accounts. Alternatively, you may choose to focus on your health and what you're eating. Shop for fresh fruit and vegetables and try to source your food locally.

Wednesday 6th

If you're looking for work, today's stars add drive and commitment to your personal toolbox. Doors could begin to open, so deepen your connections with work colleagues or your professional network. The closer your bond, the more successful you are.

Thursday 7th

Whatever your chosen goal, try to find someone to buddy up with instead of going it alone. You often find it easier to stick to a discipline or routine when you're being social as well. Be aware of who comes into your life, or take note of a conversation that inspires you.

Friday 8th

Today's potentially abundant connection could coincide with good news about work, a cash bonus or wealth flowing your way. Alternatively, you might decide to move away from a materialistic lifestyle. It's about setting things up so that your money works for and benefits you personally.

Saturday 9th

It could turn out to be a promising weekend for new developments regarding money and freedom, your health and your lifestyle. You may hear of a new work opportunity, or find a way to break free from a job or routine. This may be linked to an opportunity within your family.

Sunday 10th

It's important to close the door on work completely today, as challenging as that may be for you. The stars are encouraging you to connect with your family and to deal with any personal issues head-on. There may be an opportunity to release unwanted emotions.

Monday 11th

Whatever your current situation, this is a time to savour your close relationships and enjoy yourself with the ones you love. Put work to one side as soon as you can and concentrate on your personal life. If you have the day off from work, you're in tune with your stars.

Tuesday 12th

Try to step out of your usual routine today, even if you do so in a small way. That might mean changing your commute on the way to work, or spending your lunch hour in a different location. When you change things around, you invite magical moments into your life.

Wednesday 13th

It's time to concentrate on your work and routine. That may not come easily this morning, as you might feel tired or low in energy. You may decide to stay late at work or complete a task or project in the evening. Work with your energy levels, not against them.

Thursday 14th

There are some days when work or chores are a breeze and you enjoy what you're doing. This could be one of those days. There's a feel-good vibe, and you can gain great satisfaction from a job well done, especially if that job earns you extra cash.

. . . .

Friday 15th

Today's new moon highlights your wellbeing and lifestyle, as well as your work and routine. It's a reminder that good health means feeling well in mind, body and soul. New moon energy is great for new beginnings, especially those linked to work and your everyday routine.

Saturday 16th

Mercury switches direction today, both in your work and health sector and in the star sign linked to the body, Virgo. Favour the slower pace found in the countryside or somewhere quiet; take yourself off for a while this weekend and tap into the cycle of nature to heal and refresh.

Sunday 17th

New love could be a welcome diversion, or a lively social life could help to balance out the more mundane side of things. There's some gorgeously playful energy this weekend, perfect for a date or catch up. Be around people who lift your spirits and make you smile.

Monday 18th

This is an important week to read the small print and pay attention to the details, particularly around finances. Try not to overspend or run up debt. Integrity matters to you, so aim to deal only with people who are truthful and honest.

Tuesday 19th

You might be asked to step in and help someone out with a serious matter. If so, weigh up all the options carefully and don't get involved in anything that sounds too good to be true. When it comes to your health, be wary of expensive "miracle cures".

Wednesday 20th

Today's events could bring key developments concerning a job or position, so it's a good day to work your magic at the office and impress the boss. Other people might also admire your efficiency and eye for attention. If you're writing a CV, don't leave anything out but include every detail.

Thursday 21st

You need to find space and freedom in your life. If your home is claustrophobic or your job leaves you feeling trapped, you'll be desperate for wide-open spaces. If you're in a relationship or married, talk to your partner about a holiday or an alternative way of expanding your horizons.

Friday 22nd

You may be in a wistful mood today. It would be easy to think that there are no quick answers if you're ready for something new. Look again if this is true for you; sometimes, it only takes one small step to reignite your enthusiasm for life and set you in the right direction.

Saturday 23rd

The Sun's move into Libra today marks the equinox and the start of a new season, lighting up your relationship zone. It's time to prioritise your close relationships, both personal and professional. Don't forget your one-to-one time, as it's here that happiness and fulfilment can be found.

Sunday 24th

Arguments are good if they clear the air, but not so good if they lead nowhere and drain your energy. Bear this in mind, especially if you find yourself at loggerheads with your partner, either personal or professional. The issue may be around your future path and where you're heading.

Monday 25th

Your current good fortune is linked to what's gone before. Look back to events on/around August 10th and September 4th. News you heard close to these dates could materialise and become reality. Your potential areas of success are work and money. Be lucky.

Tuesday 26th

Love and friendship don't mix. Try to avoid getting involved in relationship drama and keep boundaries firmly in place, especially around someone who insists on being flirtatious with you. The surer you are of your self-worth, the less you'll get embroiled with silly antics.

Wednesday 27th

The pace slows right down today, and you may feel more introverted than extroverted. It's not the most confident time for you, so take a step back and do less not more. A personal issue may weigh heavy on your mind, and it could help to distinguish between what's real and what's fantasy.

Thursday 28th

Your attention to detail could go out of the window today. Do yourself a favour and keep life simple. Avoid tasks that require close attention and put off big moves for now. Schedule time for daydreaming and creative or spiritual activities. Go wherever life leads you.

Friday 29th

Today's full moon is important for you because it falls in your star sign, so it has the potential to be intense, dramatic and emotional. It might be time to stand your ground in a significant relationship. Don't compromise your wants and needs during this powerful period.

Saturday 30th

Make a definite choice about your one-to-ones: decide where your interests lie and what you're willing to put up with and what you're not. Most importantly, reignite your fiery Aries spirit. It's an ideal time to stand up for yourself and put your needs first.

OCTOBER

Sunday 1st

There's a lazy Sunday vibe today, ideal for being indulgent and taking it easy. Food may be high on the agenda. You might be cooking up a storm or entertaining friends and family. Whatever you're up to, make sure good food and drink is on the menu.

Monday 2nd

Keeping busy is a good thing now, so try not to waste time this week. Be efficient and effective, make lists, and crack on with what you need to do. Implement new habits or rules in your life and it can make a big difference to your ability to get things done.

Tuesday 3rd

Something you hear or read first thing could lower your mood. Try not to let it stop you from engaging with others and getting on with your day, especially if you have a project or task to finish. You may be working late this evening if you're on a deadline.

Wednesday 4th

The social side of life kicks in today. You'll be more interested in meeting up and talking with friends than focusing on work or chores. It's a good day for networking, marketing and selling. Any activity that involves people skills and making connections is recommended.

Thursday 5th

Talk planet Mercury moves into your relationship zone. This new phase shows where you should seek solace. If you need comfort or advice, prioritise love or friendship – it could be the nudge you need to focus less on work and routine and more on the people in your life.

Friday 6th

Comfort and caring are the order of the day. You may choose to focus on your security to ensure that you and your family are well provided for. Strong foundations in your life create a safe base. Be protective of the ones you love and invest in your home and family.

Saturday 7th

You may get frustrated with someone in your life today if they're not able to express their emotions. It's hard to know how to respond if the other person shuts off and won't let you in. Try not to lose your temper, and know that actions could speak louder than words.

Sunday 8th

You might need a positive outlook today, so put any annoyances to one side and focus on the day ahead. You're wise to do more of what makes you happy. A child's youthful spirit could rub off on you. Invite romance into your life – flirt, be social, join a dating app.

Monday 9th

Today's astrology could prove challenging. You may be trapped in a corner or caught up with a difficult boss. Do what you can, but don't keep pushing if you sense it's best to back off. Alternatively, you could decide to slam the door shut on a difficult relationship.

Tuesday 10th

Be aware that circumstances beyond your control could limit your progress, and don't run before you can walk. If someone doesn't hold you in high esteem, this could impact your career. It's important not to give in to negativity. Keep hold of your ability to fight for your rights.

Wednesday 11th

At work, look out for the person you can lean on and find out what unites you rather than what divides you. Pluto's prominence is calling you to stand up to people in power. Before you do so, reclaim your own power in a way that's authentic and genuine.

Thursday 12th

The best news this week is the fact that your planet Mars enters Scorpio, a powerful placing for the god of ambition. Mars in Scorpio is steely, determined and gives you laser focus. You won't have to give in so much to other people, and you may find that life opens up for you.

Friday 13th

Scorpio rules hidden affairs, so today's events could bring developments about money, sex, power or something taboo. Keep your cards close to your chest, be strategic, and make the right moves. It's a good time to seal a deal.

Saturday 14th

Today's new moon takes place in your opposite star sign, Libra. This suggests new beginnings regarding a relationship or a significant partnership. It's not straightforward, however, because today's new moon is an eclipse that has a hidden theme. Expect power games.

Sunday 15th

There's a witchy vibe to your stars today, which could flag up a coincidence or synchronicity when you feel inexplicably guided by life. Tap into your instincts and visit a psychic or therapist – you may have some intense emotions rising to the surface that require exploration.

Monday 16th

Get a handle on money matters at the start of this working week, especially if you know that your financial situation could be changing by the end of the month. Check out all your financial agreements and ensure you're on top of it all.

Tuesday 17th

Consider where you need to take back control in your life or be in charge. There may be a perplexing situation that requires more investigation. If so, it's time to delve deeper rather than adopt a laid-back attitude. This applies to finances, intimacy and power games.

Wednesday 18th

Broaden your horizons and look beyond the everyday. You may be working alongside someone who has a limited outlook on life or a negative attitude, which could prove frustrating for you. Be the visionary, the person who sees what's possible and goes that extra mile.

. . . .

Thursday 19th

It's easy to grow disillusioned if other people don't appreciate your vision and ideas. You may find yourself in a situation today where your beliefs are challenged or you have to make a stand on your principles. This evening, catch up with the person who gets who you are.

Friday 20th

It's worth setting up a meeting or conversation today if there's something you want to discuss, whether personal or professional. A breakfast meeting would be ideal. It is imperative, however, that a compromise is reached and that any agreement is mutual.

Saturday 21st

If you're in a situation where you've lost control or feel that other people are holding all the power, things could come to a head today. You may be unwilling to compromise your wants and needs, which could trigger the end of a relationship that's not working out.

Sunday 22nd

Communication planet Mercury moves into Scorpio, so it's time to become a super sleuth when it comes to money. Double-check everything and ensure you know exactly what you're paying out and what's coming in. Make some strategic financial moves.

Monday 23rd

The Sun's move into Scorpio is your cosmic cue to get on top of your finances and ensure that your money works for you. You might be dealing with an inheritance, a return on investment, or be renegotiating other financial ties like childcare costs.

Tuesday 24th

As an Aries, you don't always find it easy dealing with the serious side of life or delving into deep or intimate personal issues. However, this may be what's required now, especially if you're holding on to resentment or guilt. Be courageous around a personal issue.

Wednesday 25th

If you're feeling tired or under the weather, ask for help or delegate your work or chores. You may not be the flavour of the month if you do so, but you must put your needs first. Don't carry on regardless. If you have any niggles or worries, take steps to sort things out.

Thursday 26th

You may choose to pursue a more meaningful existence. Put your trust in life and tap into its mysteries. There's not always a clear answer to every problem or issue, and you may find that to be the case now.

Friday 27th

There's power in your astrology and you may be required to make some bold moves. Your decisions may not please everyone but it's time to do what's right for you. The more in tune you are with your independent and courageous nature, the easier the events of the next few days will be.

Saturday 28th

Today's lunar eclipse could trigger a conflict over money or a change in your finances, possibly involving a third party. Ensure you're on top of your accounts and don't rule out an upswing in fortune.

Sunday 29th

There's a secretive, shadowy feel to the current astrology, and you're wise to proceed cautiously. Other people have their own agenda and it could be difficult to find a compromise, especially when emotions are highly charged. You could argue over money today.

Monday 30th

The current eclipse cycle could shift your financial mindset and realign your values. Ensure you balance your head and your heart before you invest your money, time or emotions. Ideally, you should wait a little while before making any major transactions.

Tuesday 31st

You may want to socialise more today and have some fun. Check out a Halloween party or meet up with friends after work. When it comes to love, you could enjoy some flirtation in the office or down the gym. Make the most of life and embrace good times wherever you find them.

NOVEMBER
········

Wednesday 1st

Try not to compare yourself unfavourably to others today. There's an air of gossip, and you may feel a twinge of envy when you hear about a friend's new relationship. This evening, put your feet up at home or spend a quiet evening with your family. Talk less, rest more.

Thursday 2nd

Today, be around the people in your life with whom you're most comfortable, the people who know you inside out. You may crave familiarity or notice that you're seeking reassurance. If you would like a confidence boost, ask someone dear to your heart to tell you what they love about you.

Friday 3rd

You may hear a sad story today and be required to step in with hugs and words of comfort. It might be your partner who's feeling weepy or someone you work with who's had an upset. Offer emotional support rather than money if you feel the tug on your heartstrings.

Saturday 4th

You're amid some tricky astrology, so navigate your way forward cautiously through love or money issues. A key proviso is not to be extravagant or indulgent in either of these areas of your life. If you're feeling guilty about a personal situation, take a step back.

Sunday 5th

Arguments are good if they clear the air, but not so good if they lead nowhere and drain your energy. Bear this in mind, especially when it comes to your relationships. If a loved one is feeling out of sorts, walk alongside them without laying judgement or trying to fix them.

Monday 6th

Life could take you on an unexpected diversion first thing. You may end up being late for work, possibly due to a transport issue or an emergency request. Use your people skills to get on the right side of an employee or your boss. Someone in a position of influence could open doors.

Tuesday 7th

The best advice today is to engage your common sense before you invest your money, time or emotions. You may be full of creative ideas about how to improve your financial situation, but stay focused on your long-term vision and goals while keeping your money in your pocket.

Wednesday 8th

The planet of connection, Venus, enters your relationship zone. This is your cue to find the right alliances and team up with people who can help you in all areas of life. As Venus is the goddess of love, this may coincide with a welcome turning point in a close relationship.

Thursday 9th

Money dreams are worth pursuing as your psychic abilities are red-hot first thing. Investigate further and be poised and ready to act during Monday's new moon. Love is in the ascendancy. You may be delighted when someone lets you know they care.

Friday 10th

Talk planet Mercury enters your travel zone. Focus on the bigger picture in life and broaden your horizons. You might be keen to make plans and look ahead to what's next. It's a good time to do so, even if you don't currently have the freedom you'd like.

Saturday 11th

You're wise to rein in your spending and avoid impulsive moves around money. Think things through carefully before reacting to news or a significant event. Rein in your daredevil tendencies as you could be accident-prone. Less bravado, more common sense.

Sunday 12th

This could be a strange time for you. You may be feeling more introspective or secretive, which is different to your upfront nature. You may want to embrace passion and live life on the edge. If so, go for it and enjoy something secretive or hidden.

Monday 13th

Today's new moon is a perfect date to set your intentions around money and abundance. It highlights all things hidden and taboo, including sex, power, death and rebirth. You may be exploring the metaphysical side of life or delving deep into mysterious or philosophical topics.

Tuesday 14th

You might have to try a different angle when it comes to money. If you were relying on a payment that hasn't materialised, go back to the drawing board. Don't give up on a dream to travel or study but instead get inventive about funding what you want to do.

Wednesday 15th

It's easy to be disappointed if some of your long-term ideas aren't working out. Try not to fall into despair but instead turn to a good friend or a loved one for support and advice. Put your heads together and you may come up with a cunning plan.

Thursday 16th

Turn your attention towards work and career goals. When you have the right kind of leader in your life, you feel more confident about your talents and are inspired to do well. Arrange a meeting with your boss or a role model at work. You might even discuss a pay rise.

Friday 17th

Trust your insight and intuition, especially around money and finances. There's a creative vibe today, and if you come up with the right idea you could open the door to money. Part of your current learning may be around trusting your path without trying to change other people.

Saturday 18th

Today's stars indicate a confidence boost, a leap in energy and ambition. You may be passionate about asserting your identity or revealing your true self. Your courage and daring could be fierce and bring about a personal transformation. Don your cape and be a hero.

Sunday 19th

Rev up the social side of life today and arrange a get-together with your friends. When you feel good about yourself, it's easier to impress others and love could fly. If you're looking for love, ask a friend for an introduction or take yourself off to a group event.

Monday 20th

Tempers could flare first thing and you're wise to keep your emotions in check, even if you're outraged by a friend's response. What develops from a potentially tricky encounter could be revealing and help you gain a level of deep understanding or insight about yourself.

Tuesday 21st

Slow things down today. You may be on the verge of completing a deal or agreeing to a contract. If so, it's important to consider your motivations carefully and be aware of the long-term consequences. It might not mean it's not right for you, but be clear about your intentions.

Wednesday 22nd

The Sun moves into fire sign Sagittarius today. Symbolically, this feels like moving from the dark into the light. You may experience a shift on an inner level rather than via external events. Either way, this is likely to be a positive change for you and you're ready to get moving.

Thursday 23rd

You may already know that your plans aren't going to happen without some effort and things won't fall into place straight away. What you're seeking is important for your growth and personal development. Go for it, even if it means you have to overcome a few obstacles on the way.

Friday 24th

Your planet Mars moves into Sagittarius today, highlighting travel, education and philosophy – essentially, any area of life where you can broaden your horizons physically, mentally or spiritually. It could be quite the end to your year as your adventurous spirit kicks in.

Saturday 25th

Being a fire sign, feeling trapped doesn't do it for you. Be bold and seek new experiences in whatever way feels appropriate. When Mars is in your adventure zone, it's time to focus on life's bigger picture and line up some exciting activities. Don't let fear hold you back.

Sunday 26th

Doing things traditionally or conventionally doesn't fit your current astrology. Look at ways you can revolutionise your financial situation to fund your next big adventure. Acting fast could bring a brainwave. It's a great day for spontaneity and thinking outside of the box.

Monday 27th

Today's full moon is ideal for reaching out to someone in a position of influence who can help you, like a teacher or mentor. You need an activity to lose yourself in now, whether this is academic, spiritual or philosophical. Don't lose hope but be inspired by others.

Tuesday 28th

Keep the lines of communication wide open and you'll soon be full of great ideas. Talk, read, learn, debate and find the answers to your questions. If you've been at odds with a sibling or neighbour, this is the perfect day to sit down and clear the air.

Wednesday 29th

Slow things down today and catch your breath. You may be aware that it's time to touch base with family or loved ones and let them know of your plans. Sometimes, when you're on the verge of a big move, you need to know where you can find comfort and feel at home.

Thursday 30th

If you want to come up with a new way of doing something or dealing with life admin, look to your home and family. It's in these key areas of your life where you might find an unusual or unexpected solution. What this means for you may depend on your current situation.

DECEMBER

. . . .

Friday 1st

If you've been working on a new vision for your future path and have some great ideas, what you require next is a plan of action. Communication planet Mercury is in the ideal position for working out each step you have to take to reach your chosen goal.

Saturday 2nd

There's a feel-good vibe urging you to join in with a social event or line up some entertainment, but there's also a serious edge to your stars. This is encouraging you to keep on track with your long-term goals and make them happen. Balance work and play over the weekend if necessary.

Sunday 3rd

Your personal life could get in the way if someone close is being difficult or going through a hard time. A lot depends on your current situation as to whether you step in to help or take a step back. It's never easy to see a loved one upset, but keep a sense of balance.

Monday 4th

When it comes to love, you may be concerned about someone close to you. If you sense it would help them to talk their feelings through with someone, be supportive. Money and partnership are linked over the next few weeks.

Tuesday 5th

Love and relationships require commitment and a steady approach. This may be more significant for your partner than for you, but that doesn't mean it's any less important to address your relationship and consider your long-term future.

Wednesday 6th

You may feel caught in the middle at the moment and unsure of which direction to take. You might be dissatisfied with your work, or perhaps your personal and professional lives are too intertwined. Rather than seeking answers, have trust and faith that life should guide you.

Thursday 7th

If you and your partner are planning a holiday or big move, you'll be fired up and enthusiastic today. If your personal situation is at odds with your future plans, you might have to decide where your priorities lie. Make a confident move.

Friday 8th

This is an excellent day to send off a work application and plan ahead. What takes place today could promise you a lucky break. The theme of freedom runs through your work and career, your vocation and future path. Listen out for some good news first thing.

Saturday 9th

If you're in a position to offer financial or emotional support, step in to help. Love and money are closely intertwined, and there may be subtle energies playing out. Try to keep your emotions separate from a financial transaction and be savvy, not soppy.

Sunday 10th

Your finances require your attention. Listen out for miracles and go wherever life leads you. Your partner might be doing well financially, which could impact on your life. Be wary of splurging your cash because you want a feel-good boost.

Monday 11th

Schedule an important meeting or interview today. If there's someone you know who may be able to help with your plans, arrange to meet up with them this evening, especially if you're talking life admin matters. Try not to give up at the first hurdle but keep going.

Tuesday 12th

A new moon is a symbol of new beginnings, and today's is an excellent time to fire arrows high into the sky to see where they land. Explore what you want to do next and think big. Expand your life experience, broaden your horizons and embrace adventure.

Wednesday 13th

Talk planet Mercury turns retrograde today, which could halt or delay your plans. You could return to an idea or job that didn't work out the first time around. It's a chance to look at things from a fresh perspective and review your progress.

Thursday 14th

You might need a stroke of luck if there's someone you want to get hold of. If this person could play a vital role in your future, speak your desire for fortunate contact into the universe. More likely, you may find the person you're trying to reach has gone AWOL and won't be contactable until 2024.

Friday 15th

With Mercury on slow mode, it may be hard to get much done if you're working, though you may have already stopped work to take an extra-long holiday over the festive break. There could be a theme of miscommunication or misunderstandings during this phase.

Saturday 16th

If you're in a relationship or married, you may benefit from some time apart today and prefer to hang out with your friends. Whatever your relationship situation, be with like-minded people, as this could not only inspire you but help convince you that you're on the right path.

Sunday 17th

Today's events could reveal who you're aligned with and where you see things differently from other people. There may be no clear answers to a conundrum, and you're wise to let things be rather than try to force the issue. Don't lose faith if you're planning a getaway.

Monday 18th

Mercury retrograde can offer up hidden surprises. There's often a theme of retracing your steps or trying again where you once failed. For you, this is linked to work and money matters, so don't be shy in coming forward. Trust your instincts and ask for what you need.

Tuesday 19th

You may not be at your best today, and would rather be at home under the duvet than face work or responsibilities. Take it slow and try not to take on too much. Alternatively, you could get little done because you're at an office Christmas party or a boozy lunch.

Wednesday 20th

It's not going to be easy today if you're still at work and it's quiet. You may feel more impatient than usual and wonder why you're bothering. If you can spend some time working on your personal goals and aims, you'll be fired up. You need an activity that motivates you.

Thursday 21st

A loved one's behaviour could be erratic when it comes to money, but it's wise not to get overly involved. You'll get more done if you're working on your own and can close the door on all the noise. If you want to buy something special for your other half, try again tomorrow.

Friday 22nd

The Sun moves to the peak of your horoscope today. Keep aiming high and see what you can set up for 2024. Bear in mind that Mercury is retrograde, so this may be a period of research and preparation rather than an all-out attack. A little bit of magic could bring something special this evening.

Saturday 23rd

You may have some new information to hand that means your plans to travel or study are changing. See this period as a time of things unfurling rather than being set in stone. If you're in a relationship or married, be careful that neither of you get carried away with buying presents.

Sunday 24th

It's a social Christmas Eve for you as long as you don't peak too soon. If you're lacking energy or you're more tired than usual, pace yourself. You might still have your mind turned towards work or vocational matters. If you're taking on a position of leadership, be responsible.

Monday 25th

It's the ideal Christmas Day to invite everyone around to yours. Alternatively, pop round to the neighbours for drinks, or catch up with your siblings or relatives. Romance gets a look in, and one of you may be delighted with your gift.

Tuesday 26th

It might be wise to keep some of your big ideas to yourself; the last thing you want is for other people to find fault with your plans. Try not to get embroiled in a debate over ethics. Be with family or loved ones this evening and have a cosy night in.

Wednesday 27th

You may clearly see where you've come from and where you're heading as the past and future draw closer together at the full moon. Emotions could run high, especially if there's someone you're missing. Take some time out to find balance.

Thursday 28th

Your gaze is on the future, so it's a good time to invigorate your goals and plans for 2024 with new purpose. Visualise what's next for you and believe in your dreams. Even taking one small step is a start, and could help you to halt fear or disillusion in its tracks.

Friday 29th

Love has a foreign theme from today. You may be yearning for someone who lives abroad or be heading off on holiday or a romantic break. Listen to your dreams this weekend as they may point you in a new love direction.

Saturday 30th

Today's stars look more social and fun for you than New Year's Eve. If you're visiting friends or at a party tonight, you're in tune with your astrology. There might be feverish excitement about an upcoming holiday.

Sunday 31st

Look out for the person who steps in to help you or offers you a cash gift. An act of charity or abundance could make this New Year's Eve extra special. This might seem to be about financial reward, but it's also about feeling valued and increasing your sense of self-worth.

Aries

....

PEOPLE WHO SHARE
YOUR SIGN

PEOPLE WHO
SHARE YOUR SIGN

. . . .

History books and social media feeds are full of pioneering
Arians who have blazed the way for decades. From several
American Presidents, to famous footballers, Olympians,
politicians, activists, actors and YouTube sensations, discover
below which of these trendsetters share your exact birthday
and see if you can spot the similarities.

21st March

Rochelle Humes (1989), Anna Todd (1989), Ronaldinho (1980),
Deryck Whibley (1980), Matthew Broderick (1962), Rosie
O'Donnell (1962), Gary Oldman (1958)

22nd March

Nick Robinson (1995), Tyler Oakley (1989), Allison Stokke
(1989), Gaz Beadle (1988), Reese Witherspoon (1976), Andrew
Lloyd Webber (1948), William Shatner (1931)

23rd March

Kyrie Irving (1992), Vanessa Morgan (1992), Mo Farah (1983),
Russell Howard (1980), Perez Hilton (1978), Keri Russell (1976),
Chaka Khan (1953), Joan Crawford (1905)

24th March

Jim Parsons (1973), Chris Bosh (1984), Peyton Manning
(1976), Alyson Hannigan (1974), Tommy Hilfiger (1951), Alan
Sugar (1947), Mary Berry (1935), Harry Houdini (1874)

25th March

Justin Prentice (1994), Big Sean (1988), Danica Patrick (1982), Casey Neistat (1981), Sarah Jessica Parker (1965), Elton John (1947), Aretha Franklin (1942), Gloria Steinem (1934)

26th March

Louise Thompson (1990), Von Miller (1989), Keira Knightley (1985), Lesley Mann (1972), Stephen Tyler (1948), Diana Ross (1944), Leonard Nimoy (1931), Guccio Gucci (1881), Robert Frost (1874)

27th March

Jessie J (1988), Manuel Neuer (1986), Fergie (1975), Kendra Scott (1974), Nathan Fillion (1971), Mariah Carey (1970), Quentin Tarantino (1963), Mariano Rajoy (1955)

28th March

Nicolas Hamilton (1992), Zoe Sugg (1990), Alex Wassabi (1990), Lacey Turner (1988), Jonathan Van Ness (1987), Lady Gaga (1986), Julia Stiles (1981), Nick Frost (1972), Vince Vaughn (1970)

29th March

Lucy Connell (1994), N'Golo Kanté (1991), Dimitri Payet (1987), Fabrizio Corona (1974), Elle Macpherson (1964), Amy Sedaris (1961), Jane Hawking (1944), Sam Walton (1918), John Tyler, U.S. President (1790)

30th March

David So (1987), Sergio Ramos (1986), Norah Jones (1979), Mark Consuelos (1971), Celine Dion (1968), Piers Morgan (1965), Tracy Chapman (1964), MC Hammer (1962), Robbie Coltrane (1950), Eric Clapton (1945), Vincent van Gogh (1853)

31st March

Kamilla Osman (1995), Jessica Szohr (1985), Kate Micucci (1980), Ewan McGregor (1971), Angus Young (1955), Al Gore (1948), Rhea Perlman (1948), Christopher Walken (1943), Cesar Chavez (1927), Johann Sebastian Bach (1685)

1st April

Logan Paul (1995), Ella Eyre (1994), Scotty Sire (1992), Beth Tweddle (1985), Matt Lanter (1983), Chris Evans (1966), Phillip Schofield (1962), Susan Boyle (1961), Debbie Reynolds (1932)

2nd April

Michael Fassbender (1977), Adam Rodriguez (1975), Roselyn Sanchez (1973), Linford Christie (1960), Marvin Gaye (1939), Hans Christian Anderson (1805), Giacomo Casanova (1725), King Charlemagne (742)

3rd April

Gabriel Jesus (1997), Amanda Bynes (1986), Leona Lewis (1985), Cobie Smulders (1982), Nigel Farage (1964), Eddie Murphy (1961), Alec Baldwin (1958), Jane Goodall (1934), Marlon Brando (1924), Doris Day (1922), Washington Irving (1783)

4th April

Daniel Lara (2001), Jamie Lynn Spears (1991), Todrick Hall (1985), Heath Ledger (1979), Natasha Lyonne (1979), Stephen Mulhern (1977), David Blaine (1973), Robert Downey Jr. (1965), Graham Norton (1963), Maya Angelou (1928)

5th April

Rendall Coleby (2001), Lily James (1989), Hayley Atwell (1982), Timothy Bishop (1976), Pharrell Williams (1973), Bette Davis (1908), Booker T. Washington (1856)

6th April

Peyton List (1998), Rena Lovelis (1998), Julie Ertz (1992), Myleene Klass (1978), Zach Braff (1975), Paul Rudd (1969), Louie Spence (1969), Raphael (1483)

7th April

Ellarie (1986), Ben McKee (1985), Duncan James (1978), Tiki Barber (1975), Tim Peake (1972), Russell Crowe (1964), Jackie Chan (1954), Billie Holiday (1915), William Wordsworth (1770)

8th April

Allu Arjun (1983), Gennady Golovkin (1982), Chris Kyle (1974), JR Bourne (1970), Patricia Arquette (1968), Robin Wright (1966), Vivienne Westwood (1941)

9th April

Lilia Buckingham (2003), Brooke Raboutou (2001), Elle Fanning (1998), Kristen Stewart (1990), Leighton Meester (1986), Gerard Way (1977), Marc Jacobs (1963), Dennis Quaid (1954), Hugh Hefner (1926)

10th April

Claire Wineland (1997), Daisy Ridley (1992), Alex Pettyfer (1990), Shay Mitchell (1987), Vincent Kompany (1986), Mandy Moore (1984), Sophie Ellis-Bextor (1979), Roberto Carlos (1973), Steven Seagal (1952), John Madden (1936)

11th April

Dele Alli (1996), Toddy Smith (1991), Kid Buu (1988), Michelle Phan (1987), Joss Stone (1987), Stephanie Pratt (1986), Tai Lopez (1977), Jeremy Clarkson (1960)

12th April

Katelyn Ohashi (1997), Saoirse Ronan (1994), Brendon Urie (1987), Claire Danes (1979), Christina Moore (1973), Shannen Doherty (1971), David Cassidy (1950), David Letterman (1947), Bobby Moore (1941), Jacob Zuma, South African President (1942)

13th April

Josh Gordon (1991), Allison Williams (1988), Ty Dolla $ign (1985), Claudio Bravo (1983), Carles Puyol (1978), Jonathan Brandis (1976), Ron Perlman (1950), Thomas Jefferson, U.S. President (1743)

14th April

Sarah Michelle Gellar (1977), Anderson Silva (1975), Adrien Brody (1973), Robert Carlyle (1961), Peter Capaldi (1958), Bobbi Brown (1957), Loretta Lynn (1932), Anne Sullivan (1866)

15th April

Maisie Williams (1997), Emma Watson (1990), Samira Wiley (1987), Seth Rogen (1982), Luke Evans (1979), Austin Aries (1978), Samantha Fox (1966), Emma Thompson (1959), Roy Raymond (1947), Kim Il-Sung, North Korean Premier and President (1912), Leonardo da Vinci (1452)

16th April

Sadie Sink (2002), Anya Taylor-Joy (1996), Akon (1973), Jon Cryer (1965), Martin Lawrence (1965), Kareem Abdul-Jabbar (1947), Pope Benedict XVI (1927), Charlie Chaplin (1889), Wilbur Wright (1867)

17th April

Ryland Lynch (1997), Julien Solomita (1992), Medhi Benatia (1987), Rooney Mara (1985), Victoria Beckham (1974), Jennifer Garner (1972), Sean Bean (1959), Giuseppe Zanotti (1957)

18th April

Nathan Sykes (1993), Britt Robertson (1990), Rosie Huntington-Whiteley (1987), America Ferrera (1984), Kourtney Kardashian (1979), Melissa Joan Hart (1976), David Tennant (1971), Conan O'Brien (1963), James Woods (1947), Michael D. Higgins, Irish President (1941)

19th April

Joe Hart (1987), Maria Sharapova (1987), Candace Parker (1986), Hayden Christensen (1981), Kate Hudson (1979), James Franco (1978), Ashley Judd (1968), Tim Curry (1946), Jayne Mansfield (1933)

20th April

Mirandar Kerr (1983), Joey Lawrence (1976), Carmen Electra (1972), Shemar Moore (1970), Felix Baumgartner (1969), Crispin Glover (1964), Andy Serkis (1964), Jessica Lange (1949), George Takei (1937), Joan Miró (1893), Napoleon III, French Emperor and President (1808)